# BOOK OF MANKIND

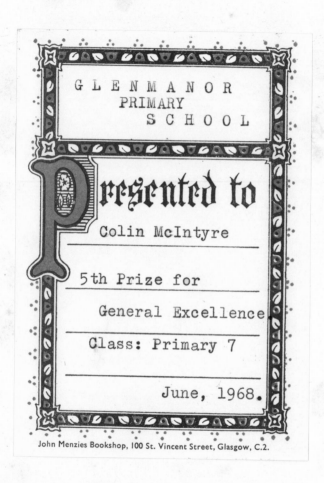

GLENMANOR
PRIMARY
SCHOOL

Presented to

Colin McIntyre

5th Prize for

General Excellence

Class: Primary 7

June, 1968.

John Menzies Bookshop, 100 St. Vincent Street, Glasgow, C.2.

# CHILDREN'S ENCYCLOPEDIA OF KNOWLEDGE

# BOOK OF MANKIND

COLLINS

LONDON AND GLASGOW

*This Edition 1967*

# CONTENTS

# CONTENTS

[*Mondiale*

On the right bank of the river Tigris is the traditional site of the Garden of Eden; and here, surrounded by a brick fencing, stands the Tree of Knowledge of Good and Evil, which is held in great awe and reverence. The group before it includes the Governor of the district, a local sheik, a police officer and an explorer.

# THE WORLD'S HERITAGE

## by M. V. JACK

Do you think of the world's progress as continuous, so that this twentieth century has the very last word on Science, Art, Literature, Music, Architecture? It would be a pardonable error to think so, but an error none the less. Progress is not a straightforward ascent, like mounting a ladder rung by rung to the top. It is more like the progress you see in the garden, where now one plant is flowering, now another. In springtime the lawns are golden with daffodils. When the daffodils die, the herbaceous border springs up miraculously tall and blazing with scarlet poppies, lupins, delphiniums, anchusas—and elsewhere at the same time the jewel tints of the rose garden are reaching their full perfection. When these too die, mingling with the frost and sunshine are the pungent autumn scents of the chrysanthemums.

That is how man has progressed in the history of the world. Now here, now there, a race emerges from barbarism, learns the arts of civilisation and develops its own peculiar culture. What that culture is to be depends, as with the plant, on the climate and soil—the natural advantages or disadvantages of its situation—but most of all on the native genius of the race. The later cultures certainly have this advantage, that they can look back on the others and learn what they have to teach.

### CHINA

We do not, of course, benefit equally from every civilisation. One of the oldest, the Chinese, has affected us comparatively little. There are many reasons for this. One is that China has always been a rather exclusive nation, even up to our own time. Another is

7

*(Mondiale*

Examples of Oriental art are shown in this picture of
a solar-clock in Peking.

that for all its great antiquity (it is at least
4000 years old) it is still alive to practise its
own arts and crafts, and science and medicine,
and need not bequeath them to anyone.

Its philosophy is Eastern and alien to our
Western ideas. The language is another difficulty—we are not much influenced by its
literature because so few of us know anything
about it. Perhaps we would have known more,
of the ancient literature at least, were it not
for a curious incident that happened long ago
—the "Burning of the Books" by the first
Emperor in 221 B.C. This early dictator was a
prince of the house of Ch'in who seized the
throne of China and planned to go on to
conquer the world. He was not really the first
Emperor, of course, but that is what he called
himself, and to make everyone regard him as
such he tried to burn all the history books in
China, so that there would be no record of
anything that happened before his time!
Among the few books saved were the works of
the great Chinese philosopher Confucius—the
*Book of History, Book of Rites* and *The Odes*, a
collection of poems and ballads some of which
even then were very old indeed.

What, then, is our heritage from this ancient

people? Not philosophy. Not literature.
Doubtless many scientific ideas have come to
us indirectly through Persia, Greece and
Rome. We have the concrete monuments such
as the Great Wall of China, which you will
read about elsewhere in this book, the Temple
of Confucius and other beautiful temples. But
our real heritage is something else, a legacy of
rare artistry—picturesque, bizarre—of painting and embroidery, fine porcelain, exquisite
carvings in jade and ivory, old arts which
China practised thousands of years ago.

Chinese painting evolved, curiously enough,
from writing. Chinese characters, as you know,
are almost pictures. They call for a great deal
of skill and some artistic ability in the writer.
So Chinese paintings were almost penned—
though with a brush! Delicate and sketchy,
they were mere outlines filled in with water-
colours. They had no perspective and did not
stand out from their background, and thus
were decorative rather than realistic. They
were done originally on wood panels—later on
silk.

Silk itself was a gift from China. As far
back as one can see into antiquity the silk-
worm was reared, and fed on mulberry leaves.

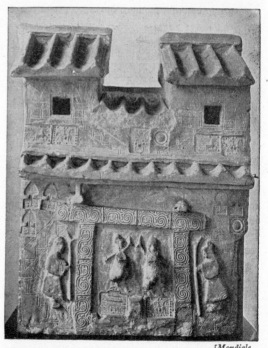

*[Mondiale*

One of the treasures of the British Museum—a Chinese
ornamental brick of about the fifth and sixth century.

Think of the science and mechanical skill which went to the spinning and weaving of rich eastern silks from the cocoon of the silk-worm—the chemistry that dyed them, the art that embroidered them in marvellous Chinese designs!

From China also came the art of landscape-gardening. It is a country rich in wild flowers, and many of these, the chrysanthemum among them, were cultivated in very early times. In Ch'ang-an the Emperor Wu-ti had a botanic garden—perhaps like the one in your own town—in the second century B.C.

## BABYLONIA AND ASSYRIA

A great civilisation arose in Western Asia which was to be of far greater importance to us than that of China. It was at least as old as the Chinese, and many people think it was the oldest in the world and date its beginnings as far back as 9000 B.C. In your Bible, in the Book of Genesis, you will read about the Garden of Eden. It was this Eden or Edin, the great plain of Babylonia in what is now called Iraq, that, was settled long ago by a race of people called Sumerians. Excavations in Iraq, and especially in the ancient city of Ur (" Ur of the Chaldees,"

[*Mondiale*

Fragment from a sculptured relief, showing an Assyrian king pouring a libation over lions at a religious ceremony.

the original home of the patriarch Abraham) give us some idea of their culture. Tombs of 3000 B.C. and earlier yield clay tablets inscribed in cuneiform (or wedge shaped) writing (an example is seen in the above picture). We know that they were able to cipher, and had an amazing knowledge of engineering and irrigation, and we can guess that it was they who first drained the marshy ground between the two great rivers, Tigris and Euphrates.

After the Sumerians came a Semitic tribe under Sargon of Akkad (2750 B.C.), who founded a dynasty. A later king, Ur-gur, built the great temple of the Moon-god at Ur. About 2100 B.C. we have the first Babylonian Dynasty, with Hammurabi as its greatest king. The very earliest code of laws in the world was made by him and inscribed on a shaft of stone, which is one of the marvellous things recovered by excavation. It was a stern but just code, not unlike the law of Moses, from which indeed it may have been derived; but while the Israelites in their little country away to the west were primarily a religious people, the Babylonians, although they had many gods, were chiefly commercial. They were what we would call

[*Mondiale*

An Assyrian sculptured relief, showing, above, a captured city, and, below, a royal procession.

"a nation of shopkeepers." They searched the known world for rich merchandise, gold and precious stones and pearls, silks and wines and costly perfumes. They had money and knew something of banking, and their merchants and shipowners made great fortunes. But in the country places, in the plains between the cities, farmers toiled on contentedly, and won rich harvests from the productive soil.

From the north was to come another race whose fortunes were to be closely interwoven with those of Babylonia. Assyria, who had long been subject to the Babylonian kings, about 1300 B.C. revolted and became the chief state. From that time for more than 800 years now one state, now the other, was to be head of the great empire—until in the sixth century B.C. it was finally conquered by Cyrus of Persia. Among its great rulers was Nebuchadnezzar II, who built for his queen the famous Hanging Gardens of Babylon.

OF the two great civilisations (which in some ways were one) that of Babylonia was not only the older but also the more important. But Assyria, with quite a different genius, copied Babylonian culture much as Rome in later centuries copied that of Greece, so that it is almost impossible to separate the two.

From Sumerian times the arts of war had been practised in those regions. A body of Sumerian soldiers in solix "phalanx," with spears and shields well in evidence, seem quite ready for a mass attack! Nevertheless it was Assyria who brought the military machine to its highest pitch. Her generals were the persons of greatest importance in the state. Her army, conscripted from among the citizens, reached a degree of military discipline which would not discredit an army of to-day. Transport and what we call Army Service Corps were well equipped and organised, and perhaps the war-chariots that thundered into battle were the precursors of the present-day tanks!

Babylonia as we have said was a country of trade and commerce. Her art was the kind of art one might expect to find in such a country —that is to say, it was designed to be *impress*-ive rather than *expressive*. It was "costly merchandise" rather than the disinterested expression of lofty ideas. Gold and jewelled bracelets and earrings, beautiful rugs, bronze work and porcelain and fine carvings—rich, colourful, enticing! A walk through the market-place of Babylon must have been a wonderful experience, but it was all too sump-tuous for true beauty. The same might be said of the houses and temples. The tiled and frescoed walls were gorgeously coloured and gilded, but the architecture was often poor and at its best was massive rather than beautiful.

A "nation of shopkeepers" may not have the highest expression of art, but there are other gifts which they may and indeed must possess. They must be able to read and write and cipher. They must understand transport and navigation, which in turn depend on engineer-ing and mathematics and astronomy. They must know all about money and banking— and it is in such modern-sounding things as these that the ancient Babylonians excelled.

The sciences of engineering and astronomy must indeed have begun in the Tigris-Euphra-tes valley—the great canals and irrigation schemes which made this region so fertile we have noted. While the Chaldeans, the "Wise Men from the East," who studied the stars, must already have learned a great deal about the heavens, about eclipses of the sun and moon and the movements of the stars and planets, thousands of years before even the simplest telescope was invented.

Babylonian literature was of a piece with all this; it included scientific works and a great many commercial documents and letters—all written on bricks! Religious writings in-cluded myths of the gods, of whom Bel was chief. The *Epic of Gilgamesh*, one of the oldest writings, is told in cuneiform characters on twelve tablets, each tablet relating a single adventure of the hero Gilgamesh. One adven-ture tells the story of the Flood as it was known in Babylon. The library of Assur-bani-pal discovered at Nineveh, contained no less than 22,000 clay tablets engraved in cuneiform characters, all of which were duly catalogued!

## EGYPT

In the garden strip of the Nile Valley, between the Sahara Desert and the mountains bordering the Red Sea, you have a civilisation nearly if not quite as old as the Babylonian. Its beginnings have been placed about 8000 B.C.! Few echoes can reach us over so vast a period of time, and of the earliest, prehistoric civilisa-tion we know very little indeed except that it existed. The next we know rather more about.

*Photos :*]
Papyrus of a famous ancient Egyptian book on religion. The expert examining it covers his mouth so that his breathing does not disturb the fragile fragments.

[*Mondiale*
A fine example of symbolical Egyptian sculpture—the Sacred Hawk, symbolising the god Horus. Note the figures and the "lettering" on the wall behind.

[*Mondiale*
From the tomb of Sennafer, at Thebes, this interesting papyrus was taken. Note that both ends of the boat are fashioned in the form of a flower, and that on the prow is the eye of Horus. All these symbols were full of meaning to the ancient Egyptians.

When the Egyptians first appear in history (at a date variously placed from 5500 B.C. to 3500 B.C.) they could read and write and already knew something of the sciences.

The great stone monuments of Egypt are perhaps its best memorial. The Sphinx, oldest of them all, is a fitting symbol of the mystery and power of this ancient arrogant people. A quarter of a mile away are the Pyramids, which you will read about in another part of this book. The Great Pyramid, the largest of these, was built by Khufu (Cheops, the Greeks called him) in the Fourth Dynasty.

Whole books have been written about the Pyramids, but still they remain a mystery. We feel that the science which built them was something quite different from the science of our own day, and in its own way no less "advanced." Do you know that the Third Pyramid is haunted by the ghost of a queen of the Sixth Dynasty who was buried there? She was beautiful, and a witch, and her name was Nitocris. Could you find a more fitting name for a witch of any age?

There are other monuments in Egypt as interesting as the Pyramids and certainly more beautiful. There is the great rock temple at Abu Simbel with the colossal figures of Rameses guarding the entrance; the Colossi of Memnon (the Greek name), one of which was supposed by the Greeks to sing at sunrise; the Temple of Amen-Ra at Luxor, largest temple in the world, with its fine "papyrus" columns shaped like bundles of reeds, or papyri; the temples of Isis at Philae—of Horus at Edfu—of Hathor the moon-goddess at Dendera. These are splendid even in decay. Massive as they are they have an almost Grecian grace of line and rightness of proportion, and we may picture what they looked like when the relief and inscriptions which cover them were gorgeously painted in the cool rich colourings of ancient Egypt.

In the valley to the west of the city of Thebes are the Tombs of the Kings. Egyptians as you know embalmed their dead and buried them with much pomp and ritual, the kings especially in very lasting tombs, either built of masonry, as in the case of the Pyramids, or cut from the solid rock. With the mummy, as the embalmed body was called, were buried various things whose "souls" might be of use

*Photos :]*          *[Mondiale*

Even in decay there is a splendour about the beautiful buildings and statues created by the Egyptians thousands of years ago. On the left is a "mural design" at the Luxor Temple; and on the right one of the famous Colossi of Memnon Statues, which has withstood the many ravages of time.

*Photos :]*                                                                 *[Mondiale*
This large and powerful statue of the figure of Prince Hemon was discovered in his tomb at Giza. The picture on the right shows part of an ancient Egyptian pulp coffin, made of papier mâché from waste paper or papyrus.

to the soul in its journey through the underworld into Paradise—food and drink, ushabti figures to act as servants, and so on. One tomb of about 2000 B.C. contained lively and realistic models of servants at work in bakehouse, granary, slaughter-house, carpenter's shop— of weavers at their looms, fishermen catching fish—of pleasure ships, houses, gardens, cattle —of everything, in fact, that the dead man had enjoyed in his lifetime.

Other tombs had furnishings that were quite priceless, very tempting booty especially to foreign invaders, and most of them were rifled long ago. Imagine, then, the world's surprise when in our own time one such tomb was found practically untouched, with all its treasure and all it had to tell, laid bare for the first time in over 3000 years! This was the tomb of Tutankhamen, opened by Lord Carnarvon and Mr. Howard Carter in 1922. It was rich and splendid beyond the wildest expectations and throws a new light on the glories of ancient Egypt.

Apart from the inscriptions on tombs and temples the Egyptians had books written on papyrus or reed paper, and often beautifully illustrated and illuminated. Their writing

was a kind of picture in itself. The characters (hieroglyphs they are called) were simplified pictures in the first case. From these they built up a literature as distinctive in flavour as their sculpture or painting. Religious papyri contained many myths of the gods, of Ra the sun-god, Isis and Osiris and the child Horus, Set, the enemy of Osiris and Hathor the moon-goddess, as well as of the sacred animals which are so much a part of Egyptian religion. There are also some legal and other documents, which help us to understand their laws.

Their most famous book was the *Book of the Dead*, designed to guide the soul through the underworld after death. Even the sun-god himself made this journey, every night between sunset and sunrise! This book—we might certainly call it one of the world's great books— was not written by any one person, but grew gradually from the beginning of the dynastic period or even earlier.

Such things are a literal heritage to the modern world. But Egypt made contributions also in mathematics, astronomy, biology, chemistry, medicine, not directly perhaps but through Babylonia, Greece and Rome. Her people had great trade and commerce, too (which helped to spread their ideas), especially in the Eighteenth Dynasty under Thothmes III, though they were not primarily merchants like the Babylonians.

Haughty as they can appear, they did not neglect the lighter side of life. They feasted, they played games (including draughts and singlestick), they played upon harps, flutes, cymbals, drums, trumpets, and they liked to watch "shows," whether dancing, bull-fighting or juggling performances, much as you might enjoy going to the circus or the cinema to-day.

## GREECE

Though Greek civilisation was not the first in point of time, yet when we think of the heritage of the past it is to Greece that we immediately look. Her legacy to us is a very lovely one—nothing less than *beauty*. From being barbarian more or less about the beginning of the sixth century B.C., the Greeks in little more than a century, seemed by instinct to light on a sort of *rightness* in everything they did which succeeding civilisations could seldom equal and very rarely indeed surpass.

It would be interesting to look for the reason

[*Mondiale*
Part of the wonderful sculpture rescued from the ruins of the Parthenon, showing a contest between man and centaur.

for this supremacy. Was it in themselves or their surroundings? Both, probably. Theirs was a small country of varied and beautiful scenery, with a pleasant climate. Here they lived simply and temperately, giving great importance to physical culture, yet allowing themselves plenty of leisure; following in fact a "Health and Beauty" cult which made life effective and pleasant. It was the very best ground in which to cultivate the arts. Had they lived among the Arctic snows or in the arid desert, or even in a city of "smoke and smirch" like London or Leeds or Glasgow, their genius would probably have developed quite differently! But when we have considered all these factors there is still one more —there is the genius itself, which flowered into something unique and perfect and altogether lovely.

Let us glance at the classic ruins which crown the Acropolis at Athens. The most famous of these is the Parthenon. This graceful temple in honour of Pallas Athene was built about the middle of the fifth century B.C., under the guidance of the sculptor Pheidias. Its beautiful Doric columns still stand, and enough of the structure to make you realise its perfect proportions and great beauty of line and ornament. Much of the statuary and sculptured frieze has been removed. The Elgin Marbles in the British Museum were brought from the Parthenon in 1812 by Lord Elgin. Its greatest glory, however, was the ivory and gold statue of the goddess Athene, done by Pheidias himself.

Nearby on the Acropolis is the Erechtheion with its fine caryatides. Lower down is the Theseion. These temples are second in beauty only to the Parthenon itself. On Olympia are the remains of the Temple of Zeus, one of the largest of the Greek temples. Here stood the colossal statue of Zeus, which, like that of Athene in the Parthenon, was a Pheidian masterpiece in ivory and gold.

Pheidias is the greatest name in Greek sculpture, but there are others such as Praxiteles, famed for the beauty and free, delightful lines of his statues of the gods, and Myron, who is known by his Discobolus, or Discthrower. A fine group by Praxiteles, Hermes and Dionysos, was found at Olympia in 1877. It is the only original work of his which we possess; others are known to us in copies.

One notable thing about Greek art is that it was fundamentally right—that it owed little to ornament. When we look at Greek literature the same quality strikes us at once—the simplicity which is not bareness but is simple because it selects just what is right and rejects what is wrong or unnecessary. Then Greek writers considered what they called the Unities, which means that they limited the compass of time, place and action to something which would be complete in itself, something to which they could do justice. The result was, in the end, a work of art.

You have heard of "Old, blind Homer," oldest of Greek poets, who wrote so long ago that we do not know if he were one poet or a great many? What we do know is that a number of traditional stories was woven by someone, or by several people, into a wonderful web, the *Iliad* and *Odyssey*, which even in translation is a thing of beauty.

Pindar, who wrote in the fifth century B.C., was the greatest lyric poet of all time. Sappho, a woman poet, also chose as her medium the lyric—so-called because it was sung to the *lyre*, which was one of the musical instruments known to the Greeks. She too was an exquisite poet with a marvellous skill in language, though little of her poetry remains.

Another part of our heritage from Greece, and not the least part, is the Drama as we know it—that is, in its literary form. There have always been actors and mummers of some kind, even in the most primitive society. It was out of such mumming in connection with the worship of the god Dionysius that Greek drama arose. One of the characters was dressed as a goat (you have heard the expression, "Playing the goat"?) and it is from *tragos*, a goat, that the word "tragedy" comes. Three famous tragic poets were Æschylus, who fought at the Battle of Marathon, Sophocles and Euripides. Only a few of their works survive, but these are still the greatest plays in the world. For dramatic power, sublimity of idea and beauty of language they have never been equalled in any literature. Aristophanes was the great comic poet. In his *Clouds, Wasps, Frogs* and other plays, he laughs at the foibles of the Athenians and shows us at the same time that the Greeks had a healthy sense of fun!

More important to the world even than its great writers are its great thinkers, and per-

[*Mondiale*

The people of Ancient Greece believed in the art of keeping fit. Here is a marathon race at the Olympic Games. Victors were crowned with laurel wreaths.

haps the very greatest of these was the Greek Plato. Born in Athens in 427 B.C., Plato was a pupil of another great thinker, Socrates, around whom he wove his famous dialogues. In one of these, the *Republic*, he has given us ideas on society and social ethics which are not out of date even now.

Does the science of the old Greeks seem rather a simple and primitive thing compared with the science of to-day? They could not fly; they had no radio or telephones; they had not even the great roads, bridges, viaducts of the Romans. When they went to war they resorted to such rather comic expedients as the Wooden Horse of Troy—they certainly had no thought of H.E. bombs or mustard gas. The truth is that such science as they possessed they used, not to make life more complex, but to beautify their uncomplicated lives.

For the abstract sciences they had more respect. They knew something of astronomy. Mathematics they studied from the earliest times, and Euclid and Archimedes were Greeks. They knew a good deal too about natural history, zoology and anatomy. Aristotle, for instance, has pictured for us the life-story of the eel, and the metamorphosis of the cicada (the golden " grasshopper" which the Athenians wore as an ornament in their hair), and other things which the scientists of our own day are laboriously rediscovering.

Certainly his *Historia Animalia* tells us some funny things. He says, for example, that there is a kind of goat that breathes through its ears, that the salamander's natural element is fire—and he describes such fabled animals as the Mantichore and the Unicorn. These, however, were the common beliefs of his day, and strange to say they were current in our own country until a few centuries ago. Aristotle taught, among other things, the beauty of living things as compared with statues, and the beauty of near things (such as flowers and insects) as compared with the distant stars. His influence, in his own sphere, was as great as that of Plato, not only on Greece but on the whole world.

Other scientists followed him, Theophrastus, the botanist, and Celsus, and of course Galen, whose writings on medicine loomed large not only in his own time (about the middle of the second century A.D.) but for centuries after. We must go back some hundreds of years, however, to find the really outstanding figure in Greek medicine—Hippocrates. Historically he was a shadowy and almost a legendary figure, and yet tradition has built up a picture that is startlingly clear and striking. It is the picture of a "Beloved Physician," the grand prototype of the family doctor, calm, confident and trustworthy—kind, humane and tireless in his efforts for the patient. Hippocrates was a skilful surgeon and his treatment of disease was thoroughly sound, but it is his character we most admire. Indeed up until our own times doctors at the outset of their practice have been required to take the Hippocratic Oath—an oath devised by Hippocrates himself to ensure the absolute integrity, selflessness and humanity which set the profession apart from almost all others.

## ROME

If the Greek civilisation exemplifies *beauty*, Rome's outstanding characteristic was *power*. Certainly there was much beauty to be found in Ancient Rome, but it did not altogether belong to the genius of the people, though it was moulded by that genius.

You know the story of Romulus, cast adrift on the River Tiber with his brother Remus, tended by a wolf until a shepherd found them and brought them up? Romulus was the legendary founder of Rome, about 750 B.C. Rome at that time must have been a very tiny state, but even then her people were a warlike race, and by the third century B.C. all Italy was in her hands. Still her power went on increasing until she was mistress of many lands—Greece, Macedonia, Spain, Carthage, Gaul and even far-off Britain.

The history of Rome is intensely interesting, but it is much too long to relate here. Rome under the Republic, under the Gracchi, under the dictator Sulla—Rome under her great emperors, Julius Cæsar and Augustus and Torajan, and Marcus Aurelius, and Nero—Rome in her proud conquests, in her decline and fall, in her final overthrow by the Goths and Vandals—you will read it all in your history books. Rome had learned to "think imperially," large-scale thinking, splendid and ruthless, and her history is a heritage to every great empire.

She was a wise ruler too, bestowing on the conquered provinces the inestimable practical benefits of her civilisation. She taught them to build houses, raise bridges, till the land. She imposed her sound laws and strong government, and introduced to them her language and literature and art. In later years Christianity itself came to us through Rome. She gave generously and without stint, and her influence on the modern world is tremendous.

Let us look at some of her gifts more closely. Latin literature has the strength and virility which belongs to the peculiar genius of the race. It has more practicality and less artistry than the Greek. This one might look for in the historians, Livy and Tacitus and others (Livy's history of Rome was a rather formidable one of 142 books!) but it is evident also in the poets.

Rome has its great national epic comparable to the *Iliad* and *Odyssey* of Homer. This is Virgil's *Æneid*, which sings the praise of Rome in recounting the adventures of the Trojan Æneas as he journeys through the Roman Empire. Virgil spent part of his life on his farm and here he wrote his famous pastoral poem called the *Georgics*. Another great poet of the Augustan age was Horace, a polished writer whose *Odes* you will some day read,

[*Mondiale*

Part of the ruins of ancient Greece, the Theatre, Athens (Odeon des Herodes, Athea). Even in ruin the building shows a dignity and grace of line, reflecting on the artistry of the builders of those far-off days whose planning and workmanship are still admired today.

*Photos :*]                                                                                     [*Mondiale*

On the left is the figure of a harpy, sculptured in marble, on a column in Rome. The impressive figure on the right is of a wolf's head in bronze, which decorated the ship's baulk in an ancient galley. These are fine examples of craftsmanship of a far-off age.

while Juvenal was a brilliant (and biting) master of satiric verse.

If Latin drama never quite rose to the heights of Greek it was none the less for many centuries the model of dramatic style. Terence and Plautus (the former at one time a slave, the latter a baker's boy) were writers of comedy. Seneca wrote a number of tragedies in addition to his philosophic writings. Both comedies and tragedies were based on Greek subjects and influenced by Greek thought.

Roman architecture and sculpture are a very important part of our heritage, though we must remember that the early Roman art was borrowed from the Greeks or the Etruscans. We are told that when Greece first became subject to Rome the Roman conquerors were themselves conquered by the beauty they saw around them. Statues and works of art of every description were carried off to Rome. Greek sculptors were commissioned to work there and Roman artists copied their productions. By and by they struck a more individual note and achieved a grandeur and dignity all their own.

The City of Rome itself is full of splendid ruins, from a few isolated columns to an almost perfect building such as the Pantheon, which is now used as a Church. Most striking of all is the Colosseum, the largest amphitheatre in the world, built by the Emperor Vespasian in A.D. 72. Here were held the terrible gladiatorial contests in which thousands of slaves and captives were "butchered to make a Roman holiday." Even in its ruined state it is an arresting monument. Here, too, is the Forum, the vast open-air assembly-hall of the people around which stood many fine statues; also the ruins of some beautiful temples and the Triumphal Arches of the Emperors, Constantine, Titus, Trajan and Septimius Severus. The Arch of Constantine, the best preserved, has a fine frieze of battle scenes.

What the Romans really excelled in was statuary. We may look at a statue of Praxiteles or Pheidias and say, "Nothing can be lovelier than this," but in Roman sculpture you have the same beauty of line and proportion with the added gift of *character*. In the portrait-busts of the Emperors, particularly of Marcus Aurelius, called Caracalla, is a true genius

[*Mondiale*

The ruins of Pompeii in Italy, the " lost city " which was brought to light again after being buried for centuries under a mountain of lava after an eruption from the volcano Vesuvius, which can be seen still smoking menacingly in the background.

[*Mondiale*

Part of the old Biblical city of Jerusalem, showing its towers and domes, and the quaint architecture which has survived through the centuries. To traverse its narrow streets is like walking through the pages of the Old Testament feeling that the well-known characters might appear at any moment.

for portraiture. They are real people rather than ideal and it is certainly the higher art.

And what of painting, you may ask—were there no Turners or Whistlers or Landseers among the Romans? The answer is that both Greeks and Romans loved colour almost as much as form. The later Romans especially often painted their interior walls with beautiful landscapes, so that even indoors you might fancy yourself on the fringes of a lovely wood or the edge of a lake; or they portrayed the adventures of Odysseus among the one-eyed Cyclops ; or depicted the Battle of Troy. Many of the houses of Pompeii, buried for hundreds of years under the lava of Vesuvius, were painted in this fashion, and when they were brought to light the colours were as fine and fresh as when they were first painted. But paintings do not stand up to the ravages of time as do sculptured stones, so that very little save written descriptions have come down to us, and in most cases the very names of the artists are long forgotten.

## ISRAEL

Let us go back some thousands of years to look at another ancient culture, that of the Israelites, whose wars and wanderings and captivities, strivings and triumphs, form the theme of the Old Testament story. They were a small nation, scarcely noticeable beside the great Empires of Babylonia and Assyria, Greece and Rome. They were not popular with their neighbours. What then, can possibly be their contribution to the world's heritage?

At a glance it is not a spectacular one. We can watch the Egyptians carving the Sphinx under a burning sky, or the merchants of Babylon haggling over their rich wares. We can picture the cool colonnaded temples of Greece, looking over pine and cypress to the sea—or the splendid fury and energy of a Roman chariot-race. But Israel, this small contentious community, had no great monuments of stone, no exquisite sculpture, no great discoveries in science or medicine to leave behind.

She had a noble literature, certainly, but it does not affect our literature so much as some others have done. We do not model our poetry on the Psalms—lovely as these are—or our drama on the Book of Job. But we *do* model our lives to some extent on this ancient people.

The Israelites, or Hebrews as we call them, could afford to let the arts and sciences go because they had something much more important to conserve. They had an intense and lofty realisation of humanity based on a right relation with God. This was their unique contribution to human progress—that they alone of the world's peoples believed that God was a Spirit, that He was one God, that He was good and just and merciful, and that men were His creation and His children, from whom He exacted obedience, not to any arbitrary whim but to His rational laws.

The Ten Commandments are the broad basis of our own moral code, and if Israel's sole claim to distinction were that she was the Custodian of the Law she would still be a mighty heritor. But in addition to the law and the very human story of a wayward and strongheaded people striving to keep it, she also gave us the Prophets, who, in language of great power and beauty and unquestioned inspiration, hundreds of years before the birth of Christ foretold the manner of His coming —who "in the fullness of time" was born into this same amazing race.

It is this that makes us feel that the Chinese and Egyptians with their hoary arts and sciences were but barbarian after all—that the Greeks, with all their beauty and philosophy, were yet earthbound, because though they brought the body, and in some ways also the mind, very near to perfection, they had only a very limited view of the spirit. And it is to this spiritual idea that we must look for the most perfect flowering of civilisation in the years to come.

[*Shepstone*

An air-view of two of the Pyramids of Giza, showing the Sphinx in the middle foreground. Below the aircraft on the left is the recently discovered fourth Pyramid, which is comparatively small but of great archæological importance. From the air, these magnificent monuments look like mere sand-castles.

The "Standing Stones" of Stonehenge were built long before Cæsar came to Britain, and can still be seen to-day on Salisbury Plain, silent monuments of days that have faded into history. What tales they could tell of their primitive builders and the lives they led in those far-off days!

# MONUMENTS MADE BY MAN

## by M. V. JACK

VERY strange and fascinating are man's monuments in stone, standing so long and so patiently, so proudly yet so pitifully—as heedless of the passage of time as though twenty or thirty or forty centuries ago were but yesterday! Wherever we find them, in splendid city or dense jungle, Peruvian forest or Pacific island, they awaken our interest and wonder by their size or beauty or mystery—but they do much more. They tell us of the past, some, it is true, in a language we cannot understand, but others again as plainly as though they spoke to us in the King's English. They are as varied and ingenious as the races who fashioned them, and as they tell of these vanished peoples they open to us whole new worlds—or rather, old worlds which to us are new and full of romance.

The most notable monument in our own country is surely Stonehenge. Everyone has heard of Stonehenge even if he has never seen it! This great ring of "Standing Stones" (only

they are not all standing now—some have fallen down) was erected long before Julius Cæsar came to Britain, away back in what is called the New Stone Age, before man had learned the use of metals.

Stonehenge stands on Salisbury Plain in the county of Wiltshire in England. It is the remains of a "cromlech," a great circle of monoliths, or huge single stones, which once supported lintel stones. Within the circle, arranged horseshoe fashion around an altar, were a number of "trilithons," each composed of two standing stones like doorposts with a third laid across to form the lintel. The largest of these, more than twenty-five feet high, fell in 1620, while John Milton was still a boy at school. Surrounding Stonehenge, like the outermost ring of a target, is a great earthwork, 300 feet in diameter, with an entrance avenue at the north-east.

In our own times scientists have learned some of the secrets of Stonehenge. They tell us that the neolithic (New Stone Age) men who raised it were sun-worshippers who observed special rites on midsummer's day, and at the summer and winter solstices. Some of the stone they used is local, some has been brought from quite distant parts of England —how, no one knows. Probably they used tree-trunk rollers and ropes woven from strips of hide, as other primitive peoples have done; and no doubt their muscles were tougher and stronger than ours, for Nature in the Stone Age gave a more-than-Commando training to her children!

In the Orkney Islands, close to another Stone Circle, a curious structure was discovered during last century by—whom do you think? A cow! While browsing on a large green mound she put her foot through the apex of this prehistoric building, a kind of hollow pyramid of which the top stone had fallen in. Like Stonehenge, this tomb (if that is what it is) is surrounded by a wide earthwork. Excavations revealed a long passage, gradually increasing in width, leading through the heart of the mound to the central chamber, which is some fifteen feet square and thirteen to fifteen feet high. About six feet from the

floor the walls begin to arch together, each of the great flagstones of which they are composed projecting a little farther into the chamber than the one below it, forming a stepped or *corbelled* vault. In each corner is a large upright monolith about three feet square at the base and nine or ten feet high, while in three of the walls hatch-like apertures lead to three small cells, roughly $5\frac{1}{2}$ to $6\frac{1}{2}$ feet long, thought to be the burial places of important people. Over all is a great cairn of closely fitted stones, the framework of the green mound which (until the cow intervened!) everyone believed to be solid hill.

What is the *meaning* of Maes-Howe? Was it a tomb or a temple or both? We cannot tell. One of the runes with which its walls are adorned (the work of Norsemen in the twelfth century) tells us that formerly it was a "Hall of Sorcery." But even then it was an ancient monument, and perhaps the Norsemen, though they may have found it a useful retreat, knew as little of its purpose and origin as we do to-day.

Malta, the "George Cross Island," lies in the Mediterranean about fifty miles south of Sicily. It is famous not only for the courage and endurance of its people (though these will

*Mondiale*

Malta is noted for the prehistoric temples built upon it, where in bygone days the gods and goddesses were worshipped with strange religious ceremonies. It is amazing to think that such large stones could have been handled and set into place without the aid of modern machinery.

*[Mondiale*

Surely the strangest of all " monuments " is the Great Wall of China which wanders up hill and down dale for no less than fifteen hundred miles. Much toil and sweat, and many tears, went into the making of it, and many people perished in the process.

go down in history) but also for the series of prehistoric temples which are built upon it. The last to be excavated, in 1915, were the Hal Tarxien temples, three structures, partly underground, of the neolithic or New Stone Age, the age which produced Stonehenge. Of the gods or goddesses worshipped there we know nothing at all. Each temple consists of either two or three oval chambers entered from a doorway composed of one or more large trilithons. Like all neolithic men, these primitive islanders loved large stones, and perhaps in the handling of these they expressed man's earliest urge to the conquest of physical forces.

One of the oddest of all monuments is the Great Wall built about 200 B.C. by the Chinese ruler who styled himself "First Emperor," and signalised his accession by the act of vandalism called the "Burning of the Books"—the destruction of all the historical records of China so far as he could find them. In order to protect China from her enemies the Huns, he planned a great wall which was to stretch across the northern border of China for no less than *fifteen hundred miles!*

You may imagine it was not built in a day! Three hundred thousand soldiers began the work, and others were added as time went on. Prisoners were sent to "The Wall" as, in later centuries, convicts to the galleys, and the toil was as bitter and rigorous, so that thousands perished while the wall was being built. On and on it wound, over mountains and valleys and across deep rivers until at last it was completed. And there it stands to-day, a solid structure of stone with brick parapet, fifteen to thirty feet high and twenty-five feet wide, with no fewer than 30,000 forts and watchtowers scattered along its length—a monument to the military genius as well as to the cruelty and ruthlessness of the "First Emperor."

Iraq, as you know, was the cradle of man's civilisation. When in 1919 scientists working there excavated the ancient city of Ur, it was indeed a romance, for here was revealed one of the oldest cities in the world. The monument of most interest is the Temple of Nannar, the Moon-God worshipped by the Chaldeans in these early times. Not much of the temple is to be seen now, of course, though we can trace its massive foundations, but one portion which still rises to a considerable height is the great tower or Ziggurat, a vast rectangular tower built in stories or stages, each rather smaller than the one beneath, like the towers children build from a nest of bricks. We are told that this is the style in which the Tower of Babel was built; and some of these Babylonian Ziggurats were very high indeed.

In the Egyptian Desert, near to the Second Pyramid of Gizeh, stands one of the most awe-inspiring of man's monuments. It is the Sphinx. The great rock-and-masonry lion with a man's head (and a king's head at that—the head of a Pharaoh of Egypt) propounds a perpetual riddle to succeeding generations of men. What is the purpose of its eternal vigil? The little roofless temple between its forepaws suggests that it was connected with some kind of religious observances—if it were not itself an object of worship.

Its proportions are colossal. As you stand

[Mondiale
A beautiful corner of the Acropolis—some of the statues on one of the temples.

in the small temple it towers above you to a height of sixty-five feet. Its battered nose is as big as a man and its mouth the size of a giant. Its air is calm and powerful, its expression unreadable.

How old is the Sphinx? It is probably at least five thousand years old, and is said to have been built by Khafra, who also built the Second Pyramid. Defaced as it is by fifty centuries of sandstorms, it shows us how successfully the Egyptians could stamp their character on the desert rock—almost, one might say, for all time.

Where would you expect to find the ruins of the most beautiful building in the world? Well, they are just where you might expect to find them—on the Acropolis at Athens. Built in the best style of Greek architecture, posed most effectively on a rock five hundred feet above the sea, the ruined temple of Athene, called the Parthenon, is the world's classic instance of beauty in building.

It was completed in 438 B.C. Within its colonnade of Doric pillars the walls were adorned with a beautifully sculptured frieze, the work of the great Athenian, Pheidias, who was also responsible for the sculptures on the gables or pediments. Indeed, the influence of Pheidias was felt throughout the whole of the Parthenon. Above the pillars were the square sculptured panels of the architraves, and over all the marble-tiled roof rose at a gentle pitch. Parts of the frieze and pediments, brought to Britain by Lord Elgin at the beginning of the nineteenth century and called the "Elgin Marbles," may still be seen in the British Museum.

Besides directing the decoration, Pheidias produced some of the statues which formerly adorned the Parthenon, notably the "colossal" statue of Athene, overlaid with painted ivory and gold. This last in its beauty and majesty rivalled his "Zeus of Olympia," which as you know was one of the Wonders of the World.

Very different from the Parthenon is the Colosseum, a monument to the power and grandeur and barbarity of ancient Rome. Both the Greeks and the Romans were fond of pleasure and amusement, but whereas the Greeks loved to strive in games and races, the Romans preferred to watch gladiators fighting with wild beasts, or with each other, to the death. For these barbarous shows they built great stone amphitheatres in almost every part of their empire—in Italy, France, Spain, North Africa, even in Britain—but the greatest and most famous was of course the Colosseum at Rome.

This vast structure was elliptical in shape, 600 feet long and 500 feet broad, rising in four storeys to a height of 157 feet. Its walls were faced with marble, and pierced with arched windows in which statues were placed. Within, great tiers of stone seats, to accommodate no fewer than fifty thousand people, rose in terraces to the blue Italian sky, while in the centre was the sanded arena where the conflicts took place.

The Colosseum was built by the Emperor Vespasian in the first century A.D., and part of its walls are still standing. During the war, after the Allies had occupied Rome, the band of a famous Highland regiment marched into the arena and for some two hours danced their Scottish dances—sword-dance and Highland fling—to the high, shrill music of the pipes.

We know that the Egyptians and Babylonians were civilised—not to mention the Greeks and the Romans—but where is the record of an ancient civilisation in the heart of Southern Rhodesia? There is none—only the faintest rumours of a culture higher than that of the natives to-day, of lost cities and a treasure of gold and ivory. Only a rumour . . . yet here in this land of the Matabele is a monument of colossal size and obviously of African inspiration, yet with a queer beauty of its own. This is the great temple of Zimbabwe, shaped like the Colosseum at Rome, with tremendously thick masonry walls rising to a height of thirty-five feet. Within, a labyrinth of broken walls suggests that the temple was a very complex structure indeed.

Everything, we note, is rounded: there are no hard angles or edges. The building itself is curved, the walls at each side of the entrances are rounded and even the steps leading to the northern gate are curved inwards. This is a rather unique style, giving an effect of smoothness which somehow adds to the apparent strength of Zimbabwe.

At a little distance is another, even stronger, structure which may have been a fort, and a high conical tower, quite solid, which was probably used as a watch-tower.

It is not only in the Old World that we find

[Mondiale
This amazing monument can be seen at Teotihacan in Mexico. It is the Sun Pyramid of the Aztecs.

great stone monuments. The New World too has its marvels in stone, nowhere more impressive than in the ruined cities of Central America. There are the richly carved temples and houses of Chitchen Itza, the wonder-city of Yucatan. There are the soaring stepped pyramids which, someone declares, are the original skyscrapers. But perhaps the most wonderful of all are the carved stone pillars, called stelæ, of Quirigua in Guatemala. Right in the heart of the jungle they rise, mysteriously beautiful but rather frightening, deeply carved with fantastic figures, quaint designs, masks of the gods and inscriptions in the ancient sign-writing. They are very much of the West, not unlike the totem poles of the North American Indians. If you can imagine a totem pole, not of rudely carved and painted wood but of stone, finely and forcefully sculptured, you will have an idea of the appearance of these picturesque pillars.

Far out in the Pacific lies Easter Island, so remote that only once a year is it visited by a ship. Here, on the shore and dotted about the grassy hill-slopes, are huge mysterious images which ever since the island was discovered, on Easter Day, 1722, have puzzled the civilised world. They are all of the same type, yet nothing like them is to be found elsewhere. The face is disproportionately large, with jutting brows shading deep eyeless sockets, long, thin nose, pursed lips and out-thrust chin. They have been called inscrutable, and certainly they have a proud, secretive, even a menacing air. The head is much flattened behind, the body shapeless (when there is a body at all—some of the statues are all face!) and the limbs barely indicated. The ears are pierced, native fashion, and have very long lobes.

There are about three hundred of these images on the island, ranging from six to thirty feet in height. One at least is sixty-seven feet tall! Some are still unfinished and attached to the quarry, which, surprisingly, is in the crater of an extinct volcano. They are all of grey puddingstone, and once they wore hats, or crowns, of red stone—great cylinders with hollowed tops in which were placed the bones of the dead.

Who or what were the originals of the statues? Were they gods or kings or ancestors of the people? In connection with the native religion a "Bird-man" is chosen each year who is "tabu" and lives the life of a hermit for his year of office. Someone has suggested that the figures represent successive "bird-men," and this may be so. Whatever their origin, these stern, sightless faces gazing out to sea are still a mystery, and no doubt they will always remain so.

ISTANBUL, on the Bosphorus in the Eastern Mediterranean—the old Greek city of Byzantium, was in the fourth century chosen by the Roman Emperor Constantine as his capital. It was called after him Constantinopolis or Constantinople. Here two centuries later the Emperor Justinian built the Church of St. Sophia. Though it is no longer a Christian church but a Mohammedan mosque, this beautiful structure still stands, and remains one of the world's great buildings.

St. Sophia was designed in the form of a Greek Cross with four equal arms. Over the square central space rose a vast dome 180 feet high. This unfortunately crashed but was replaced by an even higher one. Around were other domes—a small forest of domes, indeed, with an effect of unity and tranquillity which is quite in the best manner of modern architecture!

The Byzantine interior was much more intricate—beautiful also, but a little strange to our ideas, because it had something of the East in it. It was, however, carried out on a lavish and splendid scale, with columns of jasper and porphyry, rare marbles exquisitely sculptured, and rich mosaics on the walls and vaulted arches.

In 1453 the Moslem Turks took the church and made it into a mosque for the religion of Mahomet. They covered the mosaics with plaster, and added two tall minarets which, however, do not seem to spoil the primitive beauty of the ancient church.

Moscow is the heart of Russia, and the heart of Moscow is the Kremlin, the great fort which rises on a little hill above the Moskva River.

Its outer wall of dull red brick, 65 feet high and a mile and a half long, has five gates, and encloses not one but many buildings. Here are several palaces, including the old Imperial Palace of the Tsars, some Cathedrals (the Cathedral of the Assumption, Cathedral of the Annunciation, Cathedral of the Archangel), besides Government offices and other buildings. Much of the Kremlin is distinctly mediæval. The original "Church of the Saviour in the Wood," of which slight remains may still be seen, dates back to the early part of the fourteenth century.

The great Campanile (bell-tower) erected by Boris Godunov in 1600 still stands with all its bells, and near by is the huge Tsar-Kolokol (literally the King of Bells), which as it was broken in a fire before ever it could be hung, was afterwards used as a chapel. Tsar-Kolokol is nineteen feet high and weighs nearly 200 tons!

The Kremlin is besides a treasure-house of rare books and manuscripts, religious relics, ecclesiastical robes crusted with pearls—such a jumble of beauty and fabulous wealth and tarnished magnificence as may not be found elsewhere. For Russia is a country of vast extent and long and colourful history, and the great citadel is just the right place for her trophies.

Among the world's monuments are many memorials of grief, such as the Mausoleum of Halicarnassus in the ancient world, or the Indian Taj Mahal. Tragic as they are, they have a glory and triumph of their own which outlives the centuries.

[*Mondiale*

This striking picture shows the ruins of the famous Acropolis, at Athens, which was built in the best style of Greek architecture. Poised on a rock 500 feet above the sea, where its graceful lines are displayed to advantage, stands the Parthenon, a classic example of beauty built by man.

*Photos:*]                                                                                    [*H. J. Shepstone*

In the Egyptian desert stands the awe-inspiring Sphinx, with the Pyramids in the background, surely the most majestic monuments bequeathed to us from the Past. The statue of Rameses II in the Temple of Luxor is another powerful example. Compare the height of the statue with the figure at the side.

Above is a view of all that remains of " Babylon the Great," the once proud city of Nebuchadnezzar. It is one vast desolation of crumbling bricks and gaping holes. Below is the site of Daniel's Den of Lions at Babylon. Authorities have placed this as the spot where the lions were kept.

*Photos :]*        *[Shepstone*

*[Mondiale*

One of the world's finest buildings is the Mosque of St. Sophia at Istanbul. The interior was decorated on a lavish scale, with columns of jasper and porphyry, and rich mosaics on the walls. The Moslem Turks, who took over the church in 1453, covered these mosaics with plaster, but much of the beauty still remains.

*Photos :]*          *[Mondiale*

A lovely view, through a decorative archway, of the Colosseum of Rome. Note the wonderful figure-carving on the inside of the pillar. The great temple of Zimbabwe, in Southern Rhodesia (part of which is seen on the right) seems to have followed the same pattern as the Colosseum.

In Britain we have the Cenotaph. Cenotaph means "Empty Tomb," and that is what the Cenotaph is—a splendid empty tomb, the nation's memorial to the men who gave their lives in the First Great War.

Designed by Sir Edwin Lutyens (died 1944) and erected in Whitehall, London, the Cenotaph is a tall rectangular pylon, thirty-three feet high, standing on three broad stepped slabs and surmounted by an altar. On either side are sculptured wreaths of green stone. It is inscribed simply "To the Glorious Dead."

On November 11, 1920, King George V. unveiled the Cenotaph. Its quiet dignity and simple, tremendous significance touched people's hearts as no elaborate structure could have done, and henceforth it was to be a shrine of peace and remembrance in the busy heart of London—even of a London scarred and maimed by later wars.

And what of to-day? Architects even now are evolving new beauties—in Russia, Sweden, South America—some of which will certainly live to carry their cachet into the future.

One of the loveliest schools—if it is not *the* loveliest school in the world, was built at Rio de Janeiro in 1942. It is the Raul Vidal Elementary School designed by Alvaro Vital Brazil—an easy name to remember, since Rio is the capital of Brazil! It is of concrete, its walls pure white, its outlines simple and clean. The two wings of which it is composed are joined by a high, covered passage-way.

The entrance, of course, is from the ground level, but (so as not to obscure the magnificent view of Rio and its bay) the greater part of the school has been raised on concrete pillars. Where the first storey of an ordinary building would be there is a beautiful shady playground, with seats round the columns and cast in one with them—electric lamps set in its "ceiling." Outside this pillared space tall trees throw their shadows on the cool white walls, and beyond are the sparkling blue waters of the bay.

The climate of Rio is always warm and generally rather hot, so there is no heating problem here; but the architect has met the "cooling" problem with wide eaves, small windows on the sunny side and large airy ones on the shady side of the building.

[Mondiale

A British monument: the Cenotaph in Whitehall, London, designed by Sir Edwin Lutyens, to commemorate those who died in the first Great War. It is 33 feet high, and has a simple dignity of line, which makes it an outstanding monument in spite of its plain design.

The Australian Aborigines depend largely on the wallaby—a kind of kangaroo—for food. It is their superstitious belief that there will be an increase of these animals if a member of the tribe pours the blood from his arm vein into the hole sacred to wallabies.

[*Mondiale*

# QUEER CUSTOMS

### *by* ISOBEL KNIGHT

## WHERE IT IS POLITE TO PUT OUT YOUR TONGUE

No doubt you have often been told that it is considered very rude to put out your tongue at anyone. So it is, in this country, but if you put out your tongue in Tibet, you would be thought a very polite person.

In this strange and mysterious land which lies to the north of India, there are many strange customs. Few Europeans have penetrated into the depths of the country, and those who have, have come back with queer tales of the habits and lives of the people who live there.

When one Tibetan meets another Tibetan he does not shake hands and say "How do you do?" First he removes his funny little round hat, then he sticks out his tongue, and at the same time pushes forward his left ear!

If you were invited to a meal in a Tibetan household, you would certainly, as the guest of honour, be offered a cup of the national beverage, buttered tea. Very probably you wouldn't like it, and to avoid numerous further cups which would be pressed upon you, you would need to sip your first cup very, very slowly to make it spin out the length of your visit.

Buttered tea is made from coarse Chinese tea which has been compressed into a cake or brick. A little water is put on to boil and some of the brick is cut off and put into it. A pinch of carbonate of soda is added. A small quantity of this liquid is then poured off into a churn containing several pints of boiling water and a big lump of not too fresh butter. Salt is added and then this queer mixture is churned for a few minutes.

Every Tibetan carries his own wooden cup, and the hot buttered tea is ladled out into these. A few pellets of bread or dough are scattered on top of each cupful, and the beverage is ready for drinking. When the last cup is emptied.

the Tibetan licks it dry, and returns it to his breast pocket.

Another queer custom concerns young babies. In Tibet no new born infant is bathed. When he is three days old, he is smeared over with butter and allowed to lie in the sun for several days. As the Tibetans are a very superstitious people, astrologers and wise men are called in to consult over the important question of a name for the new son or daughter. This astrologer casts the child's horoscope and gives him a complete chart of his lucky and unlucky days. A favourite name for boys is Dorje Tshering, meaning "The Thunderbolt of Long Life." Very much grander than John or Jim, but perhaps not so easy to remember!

## WHERE MEN WALK ON FIRE

East of New Guinea and Queensland lie the beautiful palm-fringed Fiji Islands. Among this group is an island called Beqa, and on this island is a tribe of men who can walk on fire without being burned or even scorched.

Many Europeans have watched this firewalking ceremony, and all guarantee that the proceedings are absolutely above board. The fire really is red hot, and no preparation which might protect the feet is rubbed on beforehand.

A shallow pit is dug in the ground and filled up with alternate rows of wood and stones. The timber is set alight and allowed to burn for about twelve hours. The charred embers are then removed, and the red hot stones are levelled flat with poles of green wood. All preparations are now complete, and the fire walkers, usually about twelve to fourteen in number, file down and walk across the pit. They take their time, advancing slowly, even lingering on the red-hot stones for fully a minute.

Europeans who have examined a fire-walker's feet immediately after he has crossed the pit can find no sign of either burning, blistering, or scorching. When the display is over, the villagers rush forward and throw vegetables into the pit. These are cooked on the hot stones and are then eaten at the large feast which terminates the ceremony.

In the South Seas, nose boring and ear piercing are regarded as essential to beauty. Nose boring is specially popular. A hole is pierced right through the base of the nose, and into this is inserted some form of ornament, perhaps a long piece of shell or a bone. Sometimes a Melanesian dandy fancies a very large hole in each ear, so after the first piercing, the hole is made larger and larger until it is big enough to hold a ring or some ornamental circle. This fits into the extended skin of the ear, just as a monocle would fit an eye.

When a New Guinea girl wants to look her best she plaits her hair and decorates it with beads and dogs' teeth; she strings a couple of necklaces of dogs' teeth and shells round her neck, and hangs over her shoulder half a dozen pigs' tails.

In certain parts of New Guinea a youth must himself make the drum which he will carry and beat at tribal dances. The making of this drum presents many difficulties as it must be made according to custom. While working on it he must live in the bush. Often a number of boys engaged on the same work set off together. Until the hollows of their drums have been charred and scraped into shape they must on no account touch fresh water, or, so they have been warned, the hot embers used to char the drum would not glow.

During this time the only liquid the youth may drink is any water found in the stem of a banana leaf, and failing that the milk of a coconut.

Only a very small pot is allowed for cooking purposes, otherwise if he used a large pot he might be tempted to eat too much and become too fat to dance. No matter how hungry he is he must not eat any fish; if he did a fish bone might make a hole in his drum. Most important of all, no woman must see him; if she did the drum would become useless and he would have to throw it away and begin to make another one.

## WHEN TEETH ARE SHARPENED

Having a tooth drilled is not a very pleasant business, but next time it happens to you, spare a thought for the boys and girls in the northern Congo, who, when they are fifteen years old, have their upper teeth sharpened.

The process, which is done by a native "dentist," is very painful, as each tooth is chipped to a point with a sharp hand chisel. To have a row of sharp-pointed teeth is considered a mark of beauty in this part of the world.

*Photos :]* [*Mondiale*

When they reach the age of fifteen, the boys and girls in the Northern Congo have their teeth filed as a mark of beauty and seem very proud to achieve such a gruesome effect. The " fancy-dress " on the right is the battle-dress of a fourteen-year-old native of New Guinea.

*Photos :]* [*Mondiale*

Note the heavy ear-drops of the bearded Papuan and the nose-ring of the Bena Bena warrior on the right. In pursuit of decoration many native tribes are perfectly willing to undergo pain and what to Western eyes seems to be hideous disfigurement.

Another queer tooth custom is carried out among the Congo people. When a child loses his first tooth, he throws it towards the rising sun, saying at the same time, "Oh Sun! Bring me a new tooth." Then he turns to the west, and throws away a piece of charcoal, saying as he does so, "Take away that tooth of mine; it is old and I do not want it any more."

Of course, as everyone knows, a new tooth eventually grows up in place of the old one, but the Congo boy believes the sun has answered his request and brought it.

Like all the other primitive peoples in Africa, the Congo people are very superstitious. Witchcraft is the most dreaded of powers. A man will give up all his money and possessions in paying fees to a witch doctor that he may ward off his bad luck, protect him from evil spirits, and keep him in good health.

The witch doctor carries a bag of charms. These may be pieces of leopard skin, some nuts, some beads, a handful of feathers, or some small pebbles. Each one of these charms is believed to please a particular spirit. This spirit has the power to give good luck or bad luck, good health or bad health.

Families are usually large, but no parents ever count the number of their children. If they did, they believe that an evil spirit might hear them counting and take some of the children by death.

It is not considered safe to call a baby "a fine child"; an evil spirit might hear and be jealous, and the child would die.

Should anyone be so thoughtless as to forget this, the father of the child rushes to the witch doctor and pays him perhaps all the money he has in the world, to work a charm which will ward off the ill luck.

If witchcraft is suspected in a village, the headman consults a witch doctor. With the aid of his "magic" the witch doctor picks on the person he thinks to be the culprit, and the suspected man is tried by ordeal. These ordeals differ among various tribes. Sometimes the prisoner may be given a dose of poison. If he dies, or does not bring up the poison, he is guilty. Another practice is to mix a concoction of clay and grass together in a pot. The witch doctor then takes out a handful of this and throws it at the suspect. If the dirt sticks to him he is guilty and condemned to death, but if it falls to the ground he is considered innocent and is allowed to go free.

[*Mondiale*

Masked dancers of Peru with decorated dress. The feather ornamentation of the hat comes from the rare ostrich-like bird of the Cordilleras. On the right is a " gallery " of the embalmed heads of warriors in Borneo. The skulls, which are relics of head-hunting days, are smoked and painted and artificial eyes are inserted.

[*Mondiale*

A remarkable picture taken at a desert wedding of Egyptian nomads. In the foreground the bridegroom is seen singing to his bride, who, seated in her camel-box, listens from within her closed-in canopy.

## THE BRIDE TRAVELS BY CAMEL

In this country a boy would be considered very poor if he had not a pair of shoes. In Egypt shoes don't matter, but you are poor if you have not a cap, or fez. The greatest insult you can offer an Egyptian is to knock off his headgear.

All Egyptian boys have their heads shaved, and all that remains of their hair is a long tuft left on the top. This lock, they believe, is for the angel to catch if they fall over the narrow bridge which they will have to cross on their way to Paradise.

For some years the tuft is allowed to grow quite long, but when a fellow reaches fifteen or sixteen years of age, he is considered to be grown up, and the lock of hair is cut down to three or four inches, which is man-length.

In Egypt a bride and bridegroom never meet until the wedding ceremony. The marriage has all been arranged either by the man's mother, or by a professional go-between who

gets well paid for the service. Once the choice of a bride has been fixed, the eldest male relative of the bride pays over the dowry, and the marriage contract is signed. This ceremony takes place in the bride's house and is followed by a feast.

For the next eight to ten days the bridegroom sends presents every day to the bride whom he has not yet seen, and the furnishings which the bride is bringing with her are transferred to her future home. The street in which the bridegroom lives is festooned with lamps and flags, and each night the bridegroom gives a party for his friends.

The bride now makes a state visit to the public baths escorted by all her relatives. When she has bathed she returns to her old home for the last time and gives a party, where it is the custom for the guests to give her presents of money. The method of collecting this money is curious. The bride passes round a lump of henna, and as each guest handles it he sticks into it a coin. Then there is much feasting and the company are entertained by a band of hired singers. This evening is known as "henna night."

The next evening sees the bridal procession. If the bride is a town girl she rides on a donkey, but if she belongs to the country she rides on a camel with an elaborately decorated canopy covering her. If the bride's family have considerable wealth the wedding procession is long, and relatives and guests ride on camels which have been specially decorated for the occasion.

Sometimes two or three of the bride's best girl friends ride with her on the same camel. Following behind the bridal procession, and also riding camels, come the musicians, playing kettledrums, and behind the musicians come the whole village on foot.

The procession stops at the bridegroom's house, and the bride dismounts. Before she enters, however, she goes into a tent and has a meal with her female relatives. While this is going on, the bridegroom has gone to the mosque, attended by musicians and torch-bearers.

When he comes back, the bride is in his home, and bride and bridegroom see each other for the first time in their lives. If, however, he

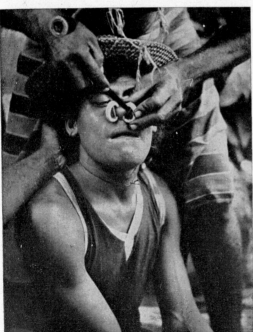

[*Mondiale*
This operation takes place in Java, where proud fathers have their noses cut so that turtle shell rings may be inserted as a sign that a child has been born.

doesn't like the look of his wife, he has only to proclaim aloud that he means to divorce her!

## SOME BEAUTY HINTS FROM BORNEO

Borneo is one of the largest islands in the world. It is peopled by a number of pagan tribes, of which the principal are the Kayans, the Kenyahs, the Klemantans, the Muruts, the Punans, and the Kayaks.

The people of Borneo are very proud of their appearance, and have many queer methods of making themselves look beautiful. A common practice among all the tribes is to pull out the eyebrows and eyelashes. Kayan and Kenyah children have their ears pierced. The girls have their lobes gradually pulled down until they sometimes reach to the collar bone. This makes the lower part of the ear into a long slender loop from which are hung a number of copper rings.

Another favourite form of elegance is to have one's teeth studded with brass stars. The teeth are drilled and brass wires, cut into the shape of stars are placed in the holes.

A flattened brow, a broad head, and a moon-shaped face are the hallmark of Borneo beauty. To achieve this, the heads of Klemantan babies are flattened with a wooden device which brings pressure on the forehead, and so forms the face into a moon shape. The pressure is only applied when the baby is asleep. Whenever the child wakens or cries it is removed.

Boys and girls in Borneo are not given a name until they are three or four years old. Then they are called after whichever grandmother or grandfather has been most fortunate in life. If, however, this does not prove a lucky name, and the child has a serious illness, the name is changed for another.

Sometimes a mother and father will choose an unpleasant name such as "Bad" or "Wicked" for their child. This, they think, will keep their little one from attracting the attention of evil spirits.

## WHERE THEY COLLECT HEADS

The natives of Borneo are head-hunters. When a tribe attacks an enemy village the heads of those killed are cut off and brought home in triumph in a war boat paddled by sometimes a hundred men, singing triumphant songs.

When the warriors reach their own village everyone is out to greet them and the heads are carried amid much rejoicing to a hut specially built for the purpose. Here they are dried and smoked.

If a chief has lately died, the village go with much ceremony to his tomb, carrying a head. When they return everyone bathes in the river. After not less than four days the heads are taken out of the hut and each man carries his trophy of war to his own home. Then there is feasting and merrymaking, including a dance by the women of the village, who hold the heads in their hands while they sway from side to side. Finally the heads are hung up in the house beside other heads taken in previous battles.

As the people of Borneo believe that spirits surround these heads, and as they are easily offended spirits, the heads are treated with great deference. A fire is always kept burning under them that the spirits may feel warm and comfortable. If a Kenyah family move to a new home, a temporary hut is built to house the heads, then when the new house is ready, the heads are transported with great ceremony.

No-one cares to have more than thirty heads hanging in his house, however, so when the removal is in progress, the family take advantage of the upheaval and get rid of any surplus ones. These are placed in a specially built hut not far from the old house, but in case the spirits who surround these heads should think they are being abandoned, a fire of smouldering logs is kept burning.

## A CEREMONY WHERE EVERYONE IS WHIPPED

A party where everyone whips everyone else seems a queer way of enjoying oneself, but it is all part of the ceremony to celebrate the growing up of a South American Indian girl of the Baniwa tribe.

For four days before the party begins the girl sits on a mat in the middle of the house. All she is allowed to eat during this time is small pieces of bread. On the fourth day the whole tribe gather round the medicine man who has prepared a bowl of special liquid. He now blows upon this to disenchant it. Early next morning the liquid is given to the girl, who is then considered of marriageable age.

[*Mondiale*

A peasant of Ecuador playing on the Rondador, an instrument which existed in the earliest times. The Indios can produce pleasant music on it.

But the ceremony is not nearly over. The maiden seats herself on a stool and is beaten with a scourge of plaited palm fibre to which the sharp tooth of a fish has been attached. The laws of her tribe are now explained to her, and she is warned that she must obey them. After she has made this promise, all the party start beating one another, not with friendly little pats, but with good hard smacks. The ceremony finally ends with a dance.

When a South American Indian dies, food, drink, money, bows, arrows, clubs, his own canoe, and sometimes his favourite animals are buried with him.

When a woman dies, her pots, pans, baskets, and other household utensils are put into her grave. The South American Indian believes he or she will want these everyday things near at hand for immediate use when they arrive in the next world. A woman whose husband dies has all her hair cut off, and she is not permitted to re-marry until her hair has grown long again.

In the case of illness, a medicine man is called in. The medicine man works his cures by a method of hypnotism. He will dance round and round his patient for hours, singing a monotonous song, and shaking a gourd rattle. During this time he smokes furiously, and takes large quantities of intoxicating drugs. At the end of a few hours the "doctor" has reached a state of complete intoxication. No matter what nonsense the medicine man talks while in this condition, the sick man and his friends believe his words are inspired by the spirits, and they obey him implicitly.

The patient meantime, has become almost mesmerised by the monotonous rattle, the sing-song voice, and the continual dancing round him, broken only by the "doctor" pausing to blow some smoke into his face or spit on the afflicted part of his body.

At last the medicine man stops dancing, bends down and sucks the portion of the body which is painful. Then he stands up and produces from his mouth in true conjurer fashion pieces of grit, bits of wood, beetles, caterpillars, centipedes, and other insects! The patient and his friends are awestruck, believing that the "doctor" has drawn these pests from the body of the sick man. Very often the invalid is so relieved to see what he thinks has been drawn from his ailing body, that he pronounces himself completely and miraculously cured.

## MAKING COLD WEATHER

The religion of the Aborigines of Australia is known as Totemism. This means that each tribe is divided into groups, each group having a special animal or object which is sacred to them. In many tribes there is a belief that men of a particular "group" have the power to make their own sacred object or "Totem" increase in number. So a "grass seed man" can make grass seed multiply, a "kangaroo man" believes he can increase the number of kangaroos, and so on.

"A rain man" is confident he can make rain, a "hot weather man," hot weather, a "cold weather man," cold weather. When cold weather is wanted, the men of the cold weather totem erect a large shelter of wooden boughs, then they light a big fire. One by one they file into the shelter and crouch down at the fire. Then they shiver and make their teeth chatter, pretending to be very cold. When this ceremony is completed, the cold weather men believe the sun will cease shining so fiercely, and the weather will become cooler.

When an Aborigine boy begins to grow up he is forbidden to eat certain foods. As he grows up and becomes a man these rules are relaxed one by one. There are so many forbidden foods, however, and the whole process of removing the prohibitions is so slow, that often a man is grey-headed before he can eat anything he fancies without breaking the law of the tribe.

Another queer custom is to mark boys and girls who are growing up with big ugly scars across the chest and shoulders. In some cases a scar is made every time a food rule is relaxed. Sometimes when a boy or girl reaches a certain age a front tooth is knocked out. This must be a painful proceeding, as of course there is no anæsthetic, and the "dentist" uses a sharp bone, which is knocked on the head with a heavy stone. One can only hope that the tooth which has been so rudely removed was one which was causing its owner pain beforehand.

## A FEAST FOR THE FAIRIES

In Rumania the country folk believe that fairies, or "fates" as they call them, appear soon after the birth of a child and determine his luck in life.

Their arrival is expected three nights after the baby is born. Father and mother are eager to please the fairies that they may bless their child with good fortune, so on the third night a table laden with choice eatables is prepared and placed under the ikon or holy image which hangs in every house.

Everyone in the house keeps very quiet, even the dogs have been sent away to friends in case their bark might frighten the fairies. A candle is kept burning near the cradle, all the doors are locked, and everybody goes to bed early so as to be asleep before the "little people" pay their visit.

During the night it is said that the fairies come and sample the feast prepared for them, then when they have finished, they write the baby's destiny on his forehead. Next morning father and mother eagerly scan his brow for any little mark on the skin which will prove that the fairies have been in the house.

When a baby is eight or ten days old it is christened. This is an important day, but considered just as important is the bathing ceremony which follows next morning.

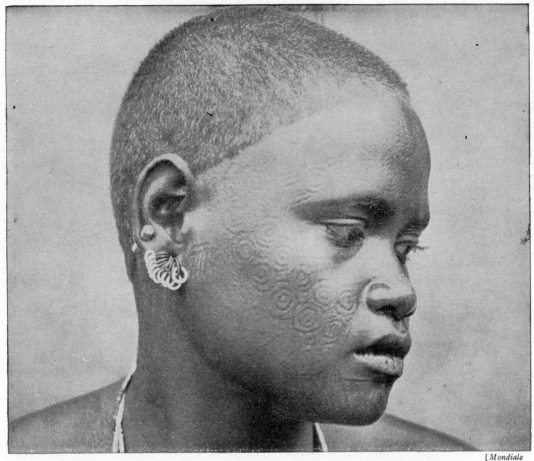

[*Mondiale*

Tattooing is prevalent in many coloured tribes and nationalities. This beauty from the Solomon Islands has had an intricate pattern worked on her face. Note also the piercing of the ears.

The baby has previously been rubbed with holy oil, and this is now washed off. Into the bath are dropped a handful of coins, and a piece of bread. This is to ensure that the child will always have wealth and food. Some sweet-basil is put in too, in order that the child may have a lovable disposition.

Weddings in Rumania usually take place on a Sunday, but the preliminary ceremonies start on Thursday when wedding cakes are prepared in both the bride's and bridegroom's home. On Saturday the bridegroom and his young men friends visit the bride's house, and on their arrival the best man recites a special piece of poetry dedicated to the bride. The bride is surrounded by her bridesmaids, beside her is her wedding cake and a bucket of water. She then distributes the cake and throws water at all the young men.

After this the bridegroom goes back to his own home, and sends his wife-to-be her wedding frock and other presents, and later in the evening the bride's dowry is taken to the bridegroom's house.

Next day the wedding ceremony takes place. Bridesmaids dress the bride and hide a silver coin in her hair so that she may never know poverty. At the marriage service two crowns made of flowers are placed one on the bride's head, and the other on the bridegroom's by the priest, and at a certain time during the ceremony these wreaths are exchanged.

Then the priest and married couple join hands and walk three times round the altar singing a special song. When the service is finished, the happy pair are showered not with confetti or rice, but with handfuls of sweets, raisins and nuts.

39

# WORLDS BEYOND THE EARTH

OUR earth is only one, and by no means the largest of the nine major planets which revolve round the sun. These planets are cold, dark bodies, shining by reflected light. They spin round the sun in their own orbits, and are kept in their places by the mysterious force of gravitation. Two of them, Venus and Mars, have an atmosphere similar to that of the earth, and astronomers believe that there is vegetable and animal life on these two planets, but none at all on the others.

Saturn, which is more than 700 times bigger than the earth, is, when seen through the telescope, one of the most wonderful sights in the heavens. It appears to be surrounded by luminous rings. These rings are composed of swarms of tiny meteors which revolve around the planet and reflect light from the sun.

Jupiter which is the largest of the planets seems to have a number of dark and light belts running across it, and dark spots appear on its surface. These spots which turn red before they disappear are probably burning gases.

In the days of long ago, when the earth was turning about four times more quickly than it is to-day, a piece of it, so say astronomers, was broken off and flung into space. This piece cooled and formed the celestial body we know as the moon. On the moon there are many lofty mountains, and by measuring their shadows, astronomers have calculated that some of them rise to a height of 36,000 feet. Owing to the lack of atmosphere these shadows are very dark indeed, and help to form the "face" of the "Man in the Moon." Other mysterious marks are probably deep valleys and the beds of ancient rivers long since dry. There is no air, and therefore no sound, not a drop of water nor a sign of life.

In olden days comets were regarded as sure heralds of disaster, bringing famine, plagues, floods and war in their train. Now astronomers have proved that these vagrants which appear in the skies for a few weeks and then vanish, are quite harmless, though some of them have heads larger than our earth and tails composed of particles of star dust, which may stretch for hundreds of millions of miles.

Comets travel at a most terrific rate, but even so, it may take one, travelling in an ellipse, as long as two thousand years to complete its circuit. About sixty comets have a comparatively short circuit to travel, and so become visible from the earth every eighty years or so. Halley's Comet comes into view every seventy-six years.

Others travelling not in an ellipse but in a parabola, are seen once and never again—they cannot curve back along their course.

Shooting stars or meteors are really fragments of a comet. Travelling at anything from ten to sixty miles a second, they become white hot, appear as bright streaks and then vanish. Usually they burn up while still in the air, and become fine dust before they reach the earth, but occasionally they descend as "meteorites" —that is, hot stones or metal fragments. These vary in size from tiny stones to huge masses like the one weighing $36\frac{1}{2}$ tons which was discovered in Greenland in 1894.

And what of the sun itself, that mighty body which holds all the members of the Solar System in captivity, and controls their movements by the power of gravitation? This sun is an enormous mass of fiery gases. Through the telescope it appears as a round, white disc dotted with small, black marks. These marks are called "sun spots," and seem to indicate that the sun is torn by terrific storms which are probably caused by cooler gases rushing in from higher levels towards the centre.

Since the invention of the spectroscope astronomers have discovered that nearly all the elements—carbon, calcium, hydrogen, etc., which are found in the crust of the earth are present in the sun also—not as solids but as gases, for the hardest stones and metals known to man could not stand up to the sun's heat.

Our sun is an enormous body with a diameter about 108 times that of the earth. It would take a train, moving at 60 miles an hour, over five years to travel round its circumference. But those little pin-points of light we call the stars are also suns, and some of them are very much larger and brighter than the one which warms our earth. One of them, Betelgeuse, has a diameter three hundred times greater than that of our sun. Of the thousands of millions of stars which can be seen through a powerful telescope, only six thousand or so are visible to the naked eye, and their distance from the earth is so tremendous that their combined light is only about a hundredth of that shed by the full moon.

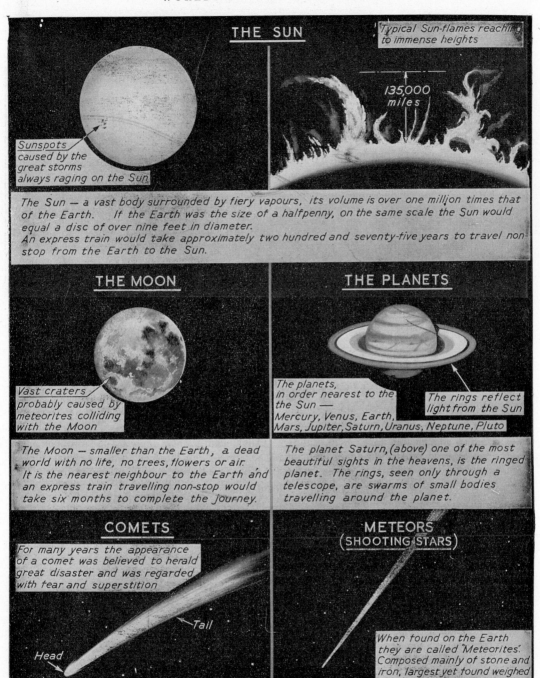

## THE SUN

Typical Sun-flames reaching to immense heights

135,000 miles

Sunspots caused by the great storms always raging on the Sun

The Sun — a vast body surrounded by fiery vapours, its volume is over one million times that of the Earth. If the Earth was the size of a halfpenny, on the same scale the Sun would equal a disc of over nine feet in diameter.
An express train would take approximately two hundred and seventy-five years to travel non-stop from the Earth to the Sun.

## THE MOON

## THE PLANETS

Vast craters probably caused by meteorites colliding with the Moon

The planets, in order nearest to the the Sun —
Mercury, Venus, Earth, Mars, Jupiter, Saturn, Uranus, Neptune, Pluto

The rings reflect light from the Sun

The Moon — smaller than the Earth, a dead world with no life, no trees, flowers or air. It is the nearest neighbour to the Earth and an express train travelling non-stop would take six months to complete the journey.

The planet Saturn, (above) one of the most beautiful sights in the heavens, is the ringed planet. The rings, seen only through a telescope, are swarms of small bodies travelling around the planet.

## COMETS

## METEORS
## (SHOOTING STARS)

For many years the appearance of a comet was believed to herald great disaster and was regarded with fear and superstition

Tail

Head

When found on the Earth they are called "Meteorites". Composed mainly of stone and iron, largest yet found weighed 36½ tons

Comets are probably composed mainly of gaseous matter. Travel around the Sun and reappear at regular intervals.
One of the most famous is "Halley's Comet". Last appeared in 1910. Next be seen in 1986.

Believed to be particles of comets, meteors become incandescent and resemble a falling star. This is due to friction when traversing the Earth's atmosphere.
Most meteors disintegrate before reaching Earth.

It is with the object of learning more about these mighty worlds beyond the eye that giant telescopes are conceived.

Transport of the coconuts from the trees to the copra station is easy when the river can be harnessed to the work. Rafts or clusters of nuts are floated downstream as in the picture above.

# THE WONDER TREE OF THE EAST

## *by* H. J. SHEPSTONE, F.R.G.S.

A TREE from the fruit of which you can produce margarine, lard, soap, candles, oils—both as lubricants and as illuminants—embrocation, perfumes, dyes, ropes, brushes, mats and a host of other useful articles, should certainly be worthy of cultivation.

Such a tree is the coconut-palm. (To speli the word with an "a," as many do, is technically wrong.) It is from the oil of its nuts and from the coir or fibre with which the latter are covered that the above named articles are made.

Gibbon, the historian, has recorded that the trunk, branches, leaves, juice and fruit of this single specimen of the vegetable world can be turned to no fewer than three hundred and sixty distinct uses.

There is an old legend that a certain king of India, wishing to send a gift to a brother monarch, sought the advice of his counsellors, explaining to them that the gift had to be something both unique and magnificent. The learned men, having put their heads together, returned to the king and reverently suggested to him that he should send such a gift as never

man had sent before him. Build a ship, said they, using nothing but the products of the coconut-palm, and freight it with all the various substances and made-products of the palm, and send the unique argosy, O King, to the royal friend.

Whereupon such a ship was built. Its planks and spars were of the wood of the palm and a tall slender trunk served for the mast. The sails were woven from the fine fibres of the husk and cables and ropes from the coarser fibres. The sea-chests, ship's furniture and couches were all made and upholstered with the various portions of the trunk, the leaves and the fruit. The eating-vessels and the drinking-vessels were carven, polished shells. The ship being ready, it was freighted with all kinds of articles all made from the coconut tree—ropes and cordages of different thicknesses, carpets, mats, rugs, brooms, brushes, boxes, baskets, oils of various kinds and perfumes. Indeed, the list included many hundreds of different articles.

Not so many years ago, in the days of our grandparents, the coconut was regarded as valuable only as a target at which to shy at fairs and on holidays. Then, when it was discovered that from its oil margarine could be manufactured as well as numerous other useful articles, coconut plantations began to spring up in all parts of the tropical world, more particularly in Malaya, Borneo, Ceylon, Africa, the South Sea Islands and the West Indies.

As a result, the cultivation of this coveted palm has been brought to a science. The botanists attached to the Agricultural Departments in our dependencies have thoroughly studied it, and as a consequence the finest and most flourishing coconut plantations are those found in British territories. What is more, they are rapidly increasing in area.

The tree, of course, only thrives in the tropics. In its wild state it is found in marshy localities along the seacoast. It was believed at one time that it could only be successfully cultivated near the sea, but the planters in Malaya, where there are now over two hundred thousand acres under coconuts, have shown that it will flourish and produce large crops of nuts in places as remote from the seashore as several hundred miles.

Fully grown, the tree attains a height of about eighty feet, with a diameter of from twelve to eighteen inches. It is marked along its entire length by the scars of fallen leaves. These marks are said to be an indication of the age of the tree, the total number divided by two representing the years. Though expert opinion differs on this point, it has always been found to be a fairly reliable method of ascertaining the approximate age of a tree.

The stem is surmounted with a crown of from twenty to thirty leaves, with the youngest nearest the centre. When fully grown these leaves measure about eighteen feet in length. The tree bears two kinds of flowers, male and

[Shepstone
Here, in the coconut garden, is a pile of the nuts, ready for dispatch to the copra station.

female. They are borne on the same stalk, the male flowers being yellowish in colour, and the female a greenish hue. The latter produce the fruit, or coconuts. The nuts are a little larger than an ordinary football, and weigh from five to six pounds apiece. Of this weight about 30 per cent represents husk. This is from two to three inches thick, and is a fibrous mass lying between the smooth outer skin and the shell. The coconuts seen in Britain are invariably stripped of this husk.

Within the shell is a hollow white kernel or nut-flesh, which, when dried, is commercially known as copra. It is the coconut's most valuable product. It is from the oil obtained from the copra that margarine, cooking fat and soap are made and also oil-cake, a much prized cattle food. The fleshy part of the nut, that is, copra, is first dried in the sun or in special kilns. It then passes to the mills where it is pressed and the oil extracted. This is an important process for the oil has to be boiled and filtered again and again, according to its quality and the purpose for which it is intended. Only the best coconut oil goes into the manufacture of margarine and lard. Desiccated or dried coconut is used by cooks and confectioners. The spirit arrack made from the coconut is used as an alcoholic basis for medicated spirits.

Copra is only obtained, however, from mature nuts. When young, the flesh of the nut is very thin and soft, and the kernel completely filled with a sweet, refreshing, white, milky beverage. As the nuts grow older this moisture or milk is partially absorbed and the cavity remains about half filled.

A peculiarity about this giant of nuts is that it easily floats in water. Coconuts have been carried hundreds of miles in the ocean, and then, floating ashore, have germinated, for the

[*Mondiale*

On the Malabar coast, in the South-west of India, coconuts flourish. Here the natives are busy loading the nuts which will be conveyed away in bullock carts. The nuts will be split and the white flesh dried, when it is known as copra. Some Negroes, skilled in the work, gather as many as a thousand coconuts a day.

trees are grown from nuts. Every year the large planters reserve thousands of these nuts for new trees, so that there is no fear of a world-shortage of this valuable and "hard-working" king of nuts.

Generally speaking, the trees do not commence to bear fruit or nuts until their fifth or sixth year. In the latter year the average yield is about ten nuts per tree, increasing to thirty in the following year, forty in the next, and thereafter the annual return is fifty to eighty nuts. Many planters get seventy or eighty and even one hundred nuts from a ten-year-old tree. This yield continues for from seventy to one hundred years, the latter being regarded as the average life of the coconut-palm. It will be seen, therefore, that the coconut has a long and useful career, and that it repays a hundredfold the small amount of labour expended on its cultivation.

When ripe the nuts fall to the ground. Curiously enough, this usually takes place during the night, which is said to account for

there being so few accidents to people on the plantations, for a six-pound coconut dropping from a height of eighty feet or more is no light object to strike a man's head. But the planters do not wait for the nuts to fall, but gather them. To accomplish this, of course, the tree has to be climbed, which is done by the coolies. Various methods are resorted to for reaching the coveted nuts. In Malaya the coolie cuts notches in the stem, and by these ascends the tree. Arriving at the crown, he holds on by one hand and with the other picks the ripe nuts. So expert are these men that one of them will gather four hundred to five hundred of these nuts in a day.

The Negroes in the West Indies, however, gather as many as a thousand nuts a day. But they ascend the tree by means of a rope-loop which encircles the stem and the picker. By this method a much more rapid ascent can be made, while both hands are free to gather the nuts and strip the tree of its valuable harvest.

# FIRE ENGINES

AN EARLY FIRE ENGINE 1735

NEWSHAM'S FIRE ENGINE 1721

AN EARLY TYPE PUMPING UP TO
40 GALLONS PER MINUTE

BED - POSTER TYPE
(LATE 18TH CENTURY)

THE FIRST STEAM FIRE ENGINE 1830. MADE
TO THROW A JET OF WATER 90 FT. HIGH
AT A RATE OF 30 TO 40 TONS PER HOUR

'VALIANT'
PORTABLE STEAM
PUMP ---1883

MANUAL FIRE ENGINE OF 1900-'PARIS' TYPE
PUMPED 70 GALS. WATER TO A HEIGHT OF
100 FT. WHEN WORKED BY TWELVE MEN.

THE FIRST MOTOR FIRE ENGINE 1903 — CAPABLE
OF TRAVELLING 25 M·P·H· DRIVEN BY A 20 H·P· ENGINE.

1928  50 H·P· FIRE ENGINE

DIESEL FIRE TENDER

WITH 'HATFIELD' PUMP - CAPACITY 250 GALS. A MINUTE.

53 H·P· RADIO EQUIPPED (PUMP ESCAPE)

MODERN ENGINES DELIVER 700-900 GALS. PER MINUTE

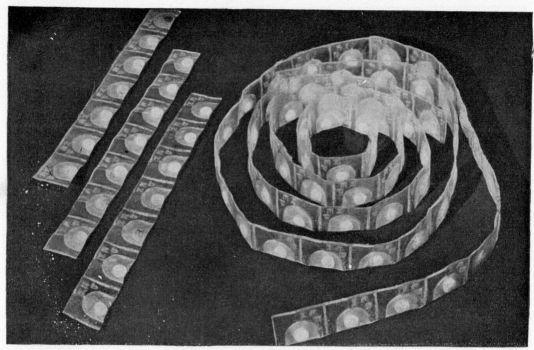

The discovery of mepacrine, a substitute for quinine, and the use of polythene, a flexible substance for packing, has done much to fight the dread disease of malaria. The "daily dose" can be torn off the film without damaging the rest of the supply.

[*Mondiale*]

# THE WAR AGAINST MALARIA

### *by* J. E. PRYDE-HUGHES, F.R.G.S.

A WAR-TIME invention, so simple in appearance that it might, without thought, be dismissed as of little importance, was the discovery of a packing which enabled an essential but unstable medicament to be supplied to troops in difficult situations. The medicament and its new packing not only saved the lives of thousands of men, and miserable illness to thousands more, but made possible operations by large bodies of soldiers in circumstances which otherwise would have been of almost insuperable difficulty.

In the jungles and swamps of the Far East one of the greatest and most deadly dangers dogging the British and Allied troops was malaria. Cut off from supplies of quinine, the one-time sovereign remedy and preventative, the Allies had to rely on the inventiveness and skill of their chemists to provide an all-essential substitute with which to fight this insidious enemy. Mepacrine was the result. This was a triumph for British chemical re-search and manufacture. But now arose the question of packing suitable for the occasions in which it was to be employed. Here again the solving of the problem was the success of British research workers in the production of the film-strip Polythene packing. Chemical and packing together constituted a great victory.

Mepacrine was produced by I.C.I. to replace quinine, from which Britain was cut off by the Japanese capture of the East Indies. It was found, however, that the Mepacrine tablets dissolved or deteriorated in the damp heat of the tropical jungles, and an entirely new method of packing had to be devised. Experts tried all ordinary materials without success. Then someone thought of the recently discovered polythene. This is the flexible plastic whose discovery by I.C.I. is one of the major scientific achievements of the past ten years. It can be produced in thin flexible sheets which are both waterproof and retain flexi-

46

bility over temperatures varying from that of ice on the one hand and boiling water on the other. Polythene had never before been used as a packing material, but the most rigorous tests showed that not only was it unaffected by tropical heat but that the mepacrine tablets wrapped in it could be left lying even in salt water for months and emerge as fresh as when first packed.

The next important problems were how to get the tablet into its individually sealed compartment in the ribbon of polythene, and how many millions of tablets a week could be wrapped. The only suitable machinery for the work available in the country was found at the works of Messrs. Genatosan, and after slight adaptations these machines were able to take a special grade of polythene film only one two-hundred-and-fiftieth of an inch thick.

Everything was ready to proceed, and soon a week's supply at a time (a strip of seven pockets) was issued to the men on the Burma front. Each day one pocket containing the daily dose could be torn off the strip, leaving the rest safely protected from air, heat and moisture in the film. And so the problem of ensuring that adequate supplies of anti-malarial medicine could be carried by the troops in the most difficult campaigning conditions, or stored for long periods in tropical countries, was solved, and many thousands of British and Allied soldiers and sailors were protected from the deadliest of foes in the Far East wars; and so, in the future, many more thousands of men will be able to live and work in comparative safety in places which otherwise would demand a high toll of sickness and incapacity.

*Indian Official Photograph, M.O.I.]*                                           *[Mondiale*
This picture, taken on the Arakan front in Burma, shows a British soldier, wounded in a skirmish with the Japanese, being helped to a dressing station. Note the dark jungle country. Here malaria is the greatest danger.

# A STUDY IN PROFILES—

Here is a very stern and classical profile, full of sombreness and dignity, and off-set to advantage by the striking headgear worn by this handsome Javan dancer.   Note the pigtail, and the decorative " breast-plate," which is part of the ceremonial regalia of the dancer.

[*Mondiale*

The Paduangs of Burma admire their womenfolk according to the length of the neck. From early childhood girls wind rings of malleable brass round their necks. As the neck is stretched, further rings are added. The women thus become giraffe-necked, some having as many as twenty rings of half-inch diameter round their necks.

# MOUNTAIN PEOPLE OF HIGH ASIA

## The Bhotias and the Sherpas

I FIRST met the Bhotias when I was exploring the Himalayas, in a rocky gorge so vertical that the path had been built over space, supported on iron stanchions like the balcony of a house. It was the month of June, and along that path came tribe after tribe of heavily-laden people driving flocks of goats and sheep, each beast wearing a harness of saddle-bags. It was the first time I had ever seen such little animals being used as beasts of burden, but each carried 24 lb. in its pair of saddle-bags, in the form of rice, lentils and flour, so it represented quite a walking cargo.

This was India, but these people looked quite unlike any other Indians I had seen. They were more round-faced, paler skinned, with red cheeks, and they wore a quaint dress of thickly-woven woollen cloaks over home-spun trousers buckled at the knees. They were cheery too, and would grin and wave to us as they herded the animals over narrow places. Strung out on these narrow paths we soon saw that they were in family parties, the well-built men with knives and swords in their belts driving the sheep, the women coming behind, fairly clanking with jewellery from bracelets to coils of beads, while huge rings dangled from their noses as they stepped it out up this path which climbs 10,000 feet in 35 miles to cross the Himalayas at 16,000 feet, where India gives way to the Tibetan Plateau, which is known as the Roof of the World.

### THE BHOTIAS MOVE HOUSE

Here, where Tibet, Nepal and India meet in a great turmoil of jagged rock spires in the districts of Garhwal and Almora, we were seeing the Bhotias moving house, for this strange people survive by using gorges such as this to penetrate the high mountains and trade with Tibet. So thoroughly developed have their movements become that families may have a share in three houses situated at different levels from the foothills to the high alps. Now, in summer, they were moving up to

Where the sheep have to carry loads. This convoy comes down the Dhauli valley in Tibet bearing Tibetan salt and borax.

their highest homes to graze their animals on the pastures laid bare by the melting of the winter snow, where the grass quickly becomes succulent.

It was only then we were able to understand why the prosperous-looking villages we had seen lower down were deserted. The people, being nomadic, had gone north into the hills and would not be back until autumn brought the threat of snow and closed the passes to Tibet in impassable drifts. Up at the edge of the snowline we found them resettling in their summer houses, the men rebuilding the damage of winter, the women busy weaving carpets or cloth in the open courtyards, or emptying grain out of the little saddle-bags carried by the sheep and goats to dry it in the sun and so prevent it rotting.

### EDUCATION

In another little courtyard a school had been set up, and an ancient autocrat was putting the children through their lessons, taking great pride in bringing the class politely to their feet when I interrupted. Then I was invited to

A Bhotia school with the teacher and his blackboard specially posed for the photograph. The Bhotias value education and the children learn writing, arithmetic and languages.

show the class the contents of my pockets; my wrist-watch, pocket-compass and camera excited the greatest interest. One little boy could even read my map. Being traders, the Bhotias know the value of education in life, so here they were studying arithmetic and Hindustani script as a third language to add to the two they already knew, namely Pahari and the Tibetan tongue. A Bhotia who cannot speak three languages is regarded as a dullard.

The word Bhotia means " Man of Tibet," and is a relic of the time when this region of the central Himalaya belonged to Tibet. They are now a hybrid people, having Indian and Tibetan blood in their veins, though their round faces and high cheek-bones have more of a Mongolian cast than Indian. But they are shrewder and more intelligent than Tibetans, and much cleaner in their personal habits. They are a people who have made life an adventure by challenging the hostile mountains which bar high Asia.

The knives and weapons we saw are their

Tibetan wool is greatly prized by the wool merchants of India for its soft quality. Here sheep shearing is in progress.

A Bhotia celebration starts to get under way. The girl with the nose ornament sings her weird song, while the oddly assorted band gives her background music and rhythm.

A high Bhotia village at the foot of steep mountains, to which access is obtained only by precipitious paths. A loaded caravan of traders returns to the village.

The dizzy heights at which these high villages are built is amazing.

protection against bandits, when, in July, they cross over to Tibet and live for eight weeks there, bartering rice, wheat, barley and manufactured goods from India for salt, borax, hides, trinkets or gold. The bandits, who live on the wild border country, lie in wait for any unprotected party, but the Bhotias give them little chance for they do not go over the mountains in ones and twos, but move together as a small army of traders, when the circumstances are favourable for the great summer journey over the mountains.

## A RITUAL DANCE

We were just in time here to see a ritual dance to hasten the rains, after which the people would plant their crops so that they could take a harvest from their fields before their sojourn in the high village was over. To a thudding drum rhythm six men and one woman wearing bright sashes danced round a burning juniper bush which gave off incense scents. Spellbound, the whole village looked on, men, women and children, as the dancers with their faces daubed with red pigment wove

Goats, with their little saddle-bags full of rice, lentils and flour, wind their way along the mountain pathway in the Dhauli valley up towards one of the higher villages.

When the trek from one village to another is over, the women settle to work weaving cloth or carpets, whilst some of the men discuss the trading trip to come.

round the " altar," going through the motions of scattering grain, or picking up handfuls of earth which they let trickle through their fingers.

Sometimes they plucked charcoal from the fire and rubbed it on their brows, their faces wearing an ecstatic look. These people are nature worshippers rather than Hindus and their ceremonies are older than religion. They have no caste barriers.

Then the woman danced a solo, throwing herself about like one possessed, her black hair swinging wildly about her as she worked herself into a frenzy. This was the first of many strange celebrations we were to see, some of them put on specially for our benefit, and once to honour us for giving medical help in this community without doctors.

## OUR DEPARTURE

A procession was formed on the day of our departure, and we marched off preceded by flute and drums, while the little boys of the village approached singing and brandishing bunches of flowers in their hands, and forming a ring into the centre of which went each little boy in turn to do his special act. One imitated a monkey scratching for fleas; another made funny faces, while one small boy got so excited in his dance he fell over himself to everyone's delight. To a volley of rifle shots we said good-bye to this delightful tribe, but we later fell in with many others.

## TRADING WITH TIBET

By tradition 25th July is the date when the men leave Milam, the last village in India, to cross over into Tibet, and their wives will not see them again before September, for they have a long way to walk and their loaded animals cannot be hurried. Travelling perhaps ten miles a day, climbing ever upwards from the gorges into the bare heights where no firewood is obtainable and only yak-dung can be used for fires, the parties spread out by day, but keep close together at night in their tents,

After the Tibet trade is over and the colder weather sets in, the Bhotias move down to autumn quarters. This village watchman stays behind with food, a hubble-bubble pipe and dogs for company, living in an upstairs room, while the snow builds up round him.

guarded by fierce Tibetan mastiffs trained to kill.

And so with a tinkling of cow-bells India is left behind and the bleak Highlands of Tibet stretch ahead, arid and dry for want of rain, but with the clearest visibility in the world in a landscape of salt lakes and fierce red and yellow colours. Living in tents and eating a kind of unleavened pancake, known as chapatties, made out of flour, together with rice and potatoes, each day brings them nearer to the villages of Gyanima, Gartok and Tollingmath which is their journey's end.

When each Bhotia meets his Mitra, as his trade agent is called, they have a charming ceremony, a kind of seal of partnership. At the beginning of their trade partnership a stone was split by a hammer, and each was given a half. When they meet they produce their separate halves and fit them together, then the Tibetan produces his goods, for he is always one year in debt to the Bhotia, and not until the Tibetan has paid for last season's supply will he be given another quota.

Despite the fact that there has, in Tibet,

been Communism since 1950, with consequent restrictions on liberty, it is interesting to record that this trade over the mountains from India has not been stopped, for the good reason that the people of Western Tibet are particularly dependent on the food the Bhotias bring, just as the Bhotias are dependent on the salt and wool for which Tibet has always been famous. Trade is carried on by barter, and this is where the Bhotia's shrewdness and higher education stand him in good stead, for he can fix the rates to his own advantage, knowing the fluctuations of the market from a study of the Indian newspapers, which he has been careful to read before entering Tibet.

## THE RETURN JOURNEY

In autumn the return journey starts. The saddle-bags on the sheep have been emptied and refilled, the yaks reloaded, and the caravan wends its way back over the tortuous passes at 16,000 or 18,000 feet, reaching its home village amidst great rejoicing in September. During the men's absence the wheat and millet have sprung up and been harvested: the potato crop is gathered, so the Bhotias celebrate with songs and dances and prepare for the big event of the year, the move down from 11,200 feet to the warmer clime of 5,000 feet.

But there is one man who does not go, because he is too old to face the difficulties of the gorges, so he becomes the village watchman with only his dogs for company. But with plenty of food and tobacco he is quite happy, though for two whole months of winter he will be confined to the house by snow up to the roof, but it will keep him alive by providing him with drinking water.

## TRADING IN INDIA

The next important event is a big Fair held on 15th November at Jouljibi in the foothills when merchants from all over India come up to compete with each other for the goods brought over from Tibet; so down the Bhotias go to the Fair. It is a time of tremendous excitement, with everyone dressed in his best clothing and over 15,000 people crowding round. Bargaining goes on hard, but not fast, from morning until night, for a business deal is a game which must never be hurried, a game of thrust and parry to be enjoyed with much arm-waving and price-cutting.

Some Bhotias, themselves heavily laden, with their burden goats ahead, climb up the mountain-side to cross a pass amidst the most spectacular scenery.

Then, when it is all over and the merchants have gone back to the plains, the Bhotias pack up their diminished stock and repair to their lowest homes to spend the winter in the temperate warmth of India, in the wooded glens which are delightful at this time of year. But the men have not finished travelling, for in December they must go down to the plains to see what they can purchase for the next season's trade with Tibet, and this will include such things as bottles of ink, fountain-pens, mirrors, lockets, pots and kettles, boxes of paints, even toys; for these are all a source of delight to the Tibetans.

And so by the end of March the saddle-bags are filled in readiness for moving up north again to the heights, the stores going first on mules and horses, then the pack-carrying sheep and goats, followed by the families, who treat every journey as a holiday.

## THE SHERPAS

These people are not of quite the same stock as the more famous Sherpas of the Mount Everest region who live some few hundred miles to the east, and who have become famous as mountaineers on great climbing expeditions. The main difference between them is that the Sherpas are really Tibetans, who happen to live on the Nepal side of the range, and are as much at home in Tibet as in Nepal, for they are pure Buddhists.

It was my good fortune to be one of the first travellers through the then unknown land of the Sherpas in 1952, and it was immediately noticeable to me what an affinity they had with the Bhotias, though they are more of an agricultural people than pure traders. On the other hand the ones who do go in for trade are exceptionally enterprising, even to the point of using air travel to visit markets like Singapore to obtain goods not available in India. Sherpas tend to be more sophisticated than Bhotias because of their close connection with Darjeeling, where they have their own shanty town.

## HOW THE MOUNTAIN SHERPA LIVES

However it is with the Sherpas of the wilder mountains I want to deal, the ones who wear pigtails and homespun clothing in the form of loose-fitting breeches tucked into the tops of long woollen boots with yakskin soles. Perched amongst the highest mountains in the world on the sides of gaping ravines, their white square houses have a wonderful attraction, and we were invited into every one to drink Tibetan tea which is made with rancid butter and salt, so that it has an oily flavour, which is rather sharp and unpleasant at first. The Sherpas drink as many as forty cups of it per day.

The houses were much more elaborate than the Bhotia houses of Kumaon, but then the Sherpas do not migrate, so they can afford to build better. Most houses were in two stories, the yaks being kept on the lower floor, the upper story being a large room with carved window frames and a fireplace in the middle of the floor. As with the Bhotias there was no furniture except carpets to sit upon, but ranged along the walls were pots and copper basins. Bales of wool and rolls of carpets showed that each house was part warehouse, and part home,

for we were offered many items for sale.

## THE SHERPAS AS MOUNTAINEERS

One significant thing about every house was the number of pieces of modern climbing equipment worn or put on show. Indeed the Sherpas nowadays can be said to live by going on climbing expeditions, and thousands of them are in demand annually by western mountaineers. They even have their own school of mountaineering led by Sherpa Tensing Norgay of Everest fame, with recognised rates of pay, so it is not surprising that the younger Sherpas prefer the adventurous life of climbing high mountains to foot-slogging across the high passes to the market towns of Tibet.

What has made the Sherpa pre-eminent as a climber is the altitude at which he lives. Inhabiting the highest valleys in the world which lie at a height of 14,000 feet, and accustomed from childhood to carrying loads to the highest pastures, these people readily become

In the Rolwaling Gorge lives a community of Sherpas completely cut off from their fellow beings, living a life of meditation. Astrologers indentified this little boy at birth as the reincarnation of a Holy Being, so he was ordained into the priesthood of Buddhism.

Sherpas crossing the Tesi Lapcha, the highest pass in the world, in the Himalayas. Accustomed from childhood to carry loads to the highest pastures, they make good porters on high peaks.

acclimatised to the rarefied air of peaks like Mount Everest, and will back-pack 40 lb. and more to 26,000 feet without oxygen. They are also tremendously hardy, as I found out when using them as porters, for they slept out at 18,000 feet in the cold of late autumn and said they were warm in their homespuns without a tent.

But even more important than their hardihood is their sense of fun and enjoyment of climbing. They love difficult ground, steep rocks, snow and ice, and revel in the struggle to go where no man has been before. They are rarely known to quarrel, and the white man who engages one finds he has not only a porter but a servant and valet as well, who will give him tea in bed, blow up his air mattress, fold his clothing, and even carry him bodily over swollen mountain streams.

## THEIR RELIGION

Being Buddhists they are a gentle people who do not take the life of even a domestic animal without the safeguard of prayer, lest they do harm to the soul of a departed human, for such is their belief in reincarnation. The

Men and women porters of Rolwaling, who carried over the Tesi Lapcha pass at 19,500 feet. The women proved to be outstanding rock-climbers.

Sherpas begin their day by praying, wherever they are, at home or in a tent, in a sing-song chant before they get out of bed, and there is nothing they love so much as a visit to their *gompa* or church.

Religion is not a solemn thing to them, but a matter for laughter and fun, whether whirling the giant prayer-wheel containing thousands of prayers written on slips of paper, or entering the semi-darkness of the *gompa* with its butter lamps burning before an image of Buddha. But each becomes solemn as he prostrates himself before the image, while a holy lama hammers a great hanging drum which booms majestically in the confined space.

But prayers are apt to be rather a marathon, as we discovered when we went to a ceremony for the souls of two women who had died shortly before, because the prayers began at eight in the morning and went on until after-noon. But there were exciting moments, especially towards the end, when the sons of the departed stood in front of the image of Buddha with bowls of corn in their hands which suddenly sprouted flames of fire. At the same

moment the most hair-raising sound burst forth out of the darkness, a roaring noise, harsh and wailing, bubbling, swelling, fading, and then becoming a piercing scream that had our scalps tingling in nervous reaction. It was not music, but a rhythm of savage wildness which came from gigantic brass horns, reed-pipes, cymbals and human thigh-bones. I have never been so powerfully moved by any sound, and it was a relief when the ringing of a little bell brought the prayers to an end. So far as I understood it the fearful din was to drive out devils.

## A HAPPY PEOPLE

We saw much of the Sherpas and journeyed with them across the highest pass in the world at 19,500 feet, over a hard and difficult route which they thoroughly enjoyed. Like the Bhotias we found them hard travellers and hard bargainers whose word was their bond. These honest men had only one dislike that I could discover, and it was an intense hatred of quarrelling. For peoples with the gift of laughter it is a natural and worthy dislike.

# NATIVE COSTUMES

SCOTLAND

FRANCE

SPAIN

WALES

JAPAN

CEYLON

IRELAND

CHINA

HOLLAND

National costumes are always picturesque and distinctive. Nine countries are represented here in their finery. These pictures provide you with material for a drawing lesson.

RUSSIA

MEXICO

MALTA

ITALY

SWEDEN

INDIA

NEW
ZEALAND
(MAORI)

ARABIA

GREECE

BURMA

LAPLAND

RUMANIA

Twelve more nations here demonstrate their respective national dress. Copying these drawings will be a
pleasant task. Look at your atlas to see where these people live.

# MODERN
# AUSTRALIA

IMAGINE maps of Australia and Great Britain drawn to the same scale; now cut out the map of Britain and you will find it fits roughly thirty-three and a third times into Australia's three million square miles of territory. Yet, spread over all this land, are just under eleven million people, little more than there are in London. Nearly half the Commonwealth of Australia lies within the tropical zone. It comprises five mainland states; Queensland, New South Wales, Victoria, South and West Australia, and the island of Tasmania. The capital cities are Brisbane, Sydney, Melbourne, Adelaide, Perth and Hobart, and the Federal Capital is Canberra in New South Wales. We are not concerned here with Antarctica, New Guinea and other islands administered by Australia.

Geologically, this is the oldest land on earth. Millions of years ago dying volcanic activity shaped the land, and in so doing it decided the way of life for modern Australians. To-day more people live along the Eastern coastline than anywhere else. The general shaping of the continent comes from a huge plateau in the west that extends over half the continent, the Great Dividing Range of the fertile east coast, the depressed central land, and the encircling coastal plains. There are few high mountain peaks, the tallest, Mt. Kosciusko, 7,328 feet, is about a quarter the height of Mt. Everest, and it is snow-clad in winter.

## RIVERS AND LAKES

Water is a great problem because of the meagre rainfall of barely twenty inches a year, averaged overall. Many rivers are dry for much of the year. Only in flood do the West Australian rivers of Gascoyne, Fortescue and others supply much water. Queensland rivers, such as the Diamantina and the Burdekin, are no more than chains of waterholes for months on end. From May to October, flying over the Northern Territory, below you are such rivers as the Finke and the Todd which are just dry, sandy beds with twisted eucalyptus growing from the middle of the watercourses.

This signpost gives some idea of the distances involved in the Australian continent.

Here and there a flash of light shows a pool below some rocky bank. In the "wet," from November to April, the rivers storm down, fed by rain on the chains of low mountains that drain into them.

The Murray River, forming part of the border between Victoria and New South Wales, is Australia's largest river. Small steamers ply its waters for eight hundred miles. Weirs and locks are being built, and eventually two million acres of land in Victoria and the two adjoining states will be irrigated by the Murray. In New South Wales, the Darling and the Murrumbidgee eventually flow into the Murray. The Darling runs across New South Wales and into Southern Queensland.

In Victoria are several small lakes, but the larger lakes shown on maps of South and Central Australia, are misleading, for most of them are thick with salt. Lake Amadeus, below Alice Springs, as seen from the air seems to split the land in two with its length of over a hundred and fifty miles. It is blue-white, like watered milk, and heavy with salt, for it is the last tired remnant of the inland sea that once covered the central land.

## SUB-ARTESIAN BORES

Other sources of water compensate for the sparse rainfall. Artesian basins lie under a third of the continent. In Queensland about 3,000 are in use. The water is forced up by underground pressure; but with sub-artesian bores, of which there are 10,000, water has to be pumped into storage tanks. The bores are usually strongly mineral and useless for plant growth, but thirsty sheep and cattle can drink it. The hot, medicinal bores smell of sulphur and people both bath in it and drink it for their complaints. The flow is tremendous, one bore pours 1,300,000 gallons per day, year after year, all from the great oceans that must lie beneath the land.

## WATER CONSERVATION

Water for the big cities is mainly conserved in dams. There are other projects too, such as in Western Australia where " water trains " are in summer use. Weirs, dams and pipelines are being extended, and dams such as Burrin-juck, are part of projects like the Snowy Mountains Scheme, of which the first stage, completed in 1961, already supplies hydro-electricity to Victoria and N.S.W. Australia's future depends largely on solving drought and flood problems, both of which cause untold hardship to settlers.

## CATTLE STATIONS

Since 1945, over four million migrants have gone to Australia to add their skill to the nation's economy. All Australia's biggest cities are on the coastal strip, and the majority of people live in the cities. Before the land can be fully peopled, the farthest corners of inhospitable areas must be made habitable. Wool, shorn from 165,000,000 sheep, is still the chief primary industry. Cattle breeding has expanded into the empty lands of the Northern Territory. There the cattle stations (ranches) are enormous. Victoria River Downs is probably the largest cattle run in the world with its 11,262 square miles of land

Guthega Dam, 5,000 ft. above sea level was the first major project to come into commercial operation in the Snowy Mountains scheme. The associated power house will eventually have an output of 90,000 kw.

running 100,000 cattle. In 1957 eight thousand cattle were sold from there alone.

Darwin is the capital of the Northern Territory, land of the future. In the geographical centre of Australia is the town of Alice Springs, white houses set in the greenery of citrus fruit trees, it is the centre of the mining areas and the huge cattle stations. Flying over the Territory you can see why it is called the place of the " great Australian loneliness," one looks down on red, red earth patterned in circles of bright green spinifex bushes. The earth looks like a richly embroidered cloth spread across land so vast that people call it "nothing but miles of nothing." The untapped resources of the central territory of Australia, still remain to be discovered, and to-morrow it may challenge the more easily colonised east coast.

A typical sugar-cane field shortly after replanting. The man in the picture is " putting in the misses."

Beef cattle from this " red heart " of the continent may have to travel two thousand miles for slaughtering or shipping. On Cape York, one pastoral company uses post-war landing craft to take their cattle to ports en route for the Philippines; and air transport is planned to New Guinea where, to enable the same company to back-load the aircraft, they intend growing tea and coffee.

## RUSTLING OF CATTLE

The Australian has endless opportunities for enterprise. Experiments in crossing Brahmins (water buffalo) and shorthorns or Herefords have produced the " Droughtmaster " in the north and a similar cross, the " Santa Gertrudis," was introduced into New South Wales from the U.S.A. in 1952. They are both successful. These cattle are suited to the intense heat of the Northern Territory and are disease-resistant and fatten well. The romance of great cattlelands is not confined to the Wild West of America. Early in 1957 police smashed a gang of rustlers in the Queensland Gulf Country, recovering seven hundred head of stolen cattle which had been driven into secret ravines a hundred miles away.

## AFTERMATH OF WAR

The war left a welcome mileage of bitumen roads in North Queensland, along which diesel road trains and huge trucks move the beef cattle. In meat-preservation, experiments with ultra-violet light show promise. The first School for Cattlemen opened at Canobie, near Cloncurry, about two years ago.

At one time horses were bred for the Indian Army. Now barely 600,000 horses remain throughout Australia. In the north great mobs of wild horses called brumbies, as well as herds of donkeys, camels and buffaloes, roam the land.

## MAIN SOURCES OF REVENUE

Agriculture is of primary importance, wheat is the most extensive crop for export. Oats, barley and all types of hay are grown. The tinning and preservation of fruit crops is a big industry. Sugar-cane, grown mainly in Queensland, helps to develop large tropical areas and the Government does not allow imported sugar. It is grown with all-white labour, which is unique in the sugar industry. Scientists improve many of the milling processes. Sometimes " improvements " backfire; because rats lurked among the growing cane, huge toads were imported, now the toads are a menace, eating small mammals and moving southward out of the cane-fields.

Other crops are cotton, rice, tobacco and grapes. Wines are an increasing export. Science in prospecting has opened up the mineral wealth of Australia. Now gold, silver, lead and iron are not the most important metals. Bauxite, the ore of aluminium, once rare, is found in quantity, and whole townships built to exploit it are projected for the Cape York areas. The old prospector with his pick and his sieve has given place to the man with the Geiger counter. Large uranium deposits have been found at Rum Jungle, the Mary Kathleen, and other fields.

Unusual minerals have been discovered in unusual places. One Queensland company has a fifty-foot steel vessel equipped to test for minerals twenty feet into the ocean bed, at a depth of two hundred feet below the surface. On the Gold Coast, a rich tourist resort sixty-five miles from Brisbane, tons of valuable rutile, a mineral used in alloys, has been extracted from the beach sands. Rutile looks like black specks and gives the golden sand weight, so that when the rutile is removed, the sand becomes light and windblown. Another company has permits to prospect for rutile over sixty-two square miles of ocean bed off the Queensland coast.

Because of the long sea-routes from oil-bearing areas, the discovery of oil in Western Australia has touched off prospecting elsewhere, particularly in South-west Queensland and on the Southern Australian border.

## SMALL INDUSTRIES

That cold fire gouged from the earth, the black opal, is worked out at Lightning Ridge in New South Wales, the only place it was found. Now that unskilled workers can make big money they do not go prospecting any more, and no new fields of these regal stones have been found. The pale opals are still mined by " gougers " at White Cliffs in New South Wales and at Coober Pedy in Southern Australia where the small community lives and works underground to avoid the intense heat.

There are innumerable small industries, such as the honey-collecting of itinerant bee-keepers who travel about the eastern states; the pearl-shell and trochus industry at Broome

Australia's first nuclear reactor, known as HIFAR (high Flux Australian Reactor).

and Darwin; buffalo-shooting for hides in the Territory, and crocodile shooting by men who, a few years ago brought in 10,000 skins a season for the manufacture of handbags, shoes and other articles. These men have defeated themselves by their own greed, to-day the crocodiles round Darwin are almost shot-out.

The fishing industry is not a large one. There are no lobsters in Australian waters, but crayfish are popular. Supplies of giant prawns were discovered recently. Barramundi, kingfish, and garfish have good sales.

## WONDERS OF THE REEF

The Great Barrier Reef, following the east coast for 1,250 miles, is the greatest of all coral reefs and one of the wonders of the world. During the winter many thousands of tourists go there, but there is room for thousands more, and excellent accommodation offers at such places as Cairns. Sixteen miles from there Green Island rises from the outer reef, and it has a unique underwater observatory where visitors can see the natural marvels of the corals and watch the brilliant fish swimming through it.

Departure of a Vickers Viscount of Trans-Australia Airlines from the Kingsford-Smith Airport at Mascot, four miles south of the centre of Sydney.

## AIR TRAVEL

"Cornerstone" industries such as engineering, ironfounding, metal extraction, shipbuilding, machinery, car and aircraft building, are all expanding rapidly. Australia is one of the most air-minded of countries. The vast, uninhabited tracts are criss-crossed not only by the big air-lines such as Trans-Australia Airways, but also by numerous charter planes and the privately-owned aircraft of graziers. Airstrips for landing in the wilderness are as common as are traffic islands in Piccadilly.

## RESEARCH AND TECHNICAL ORGANISATION

Science, fairy godmother at the christening of thousands of new projects, stems from the Commonwealths Scientific Organisations for the study of industrial chemistry, animal health, food preservation, irrigation, wool and textile research, and hundreds of other lines that lead to new techniques and discoveries.

## TASMANIA

Tasmania, the smallest state, two hundred

Australia's engineering industry is expanding rapidly. Here you see shells of car bodies ready for conversion into complete vehicles.

A "jumbo" mechanical miner burrowing through a mountain on the vast Snowy Mountain Hydro-Electric scheme, which was begun in 1949—to be completed in about 20 years.

miles south of the mainland is a shield-shaped island about as big as Scotland. It is divided from the mainland by Bass Strait. Its climate is moist and cool and it has no drought problem. Northwards lies most of the agricultural and farming land. Dairying is a flourishing industry, sheep are bred for mutton as well as for wool, but especially for pedigreed strains. Tasmanian apples are world famous. Oats, wheat and potatoes are other crops grown for home use.

Most of the west of the island is inaccessible, with thickly-overgrown mountains and gorges. In the high centre of the island lie many lakes with hydro-electric schemes based on them. The largest lake is the Great Lake, 3,000 feet above sea-level. Hobart, the capital is on the Derwent River, and Launceston is the chief shipping port. There are big National Parks, snow sports in winter; and, in spite of its small size the island keeps its secrets, for

instance, the River Gordon, has never been fully explored.

Pulp-mills for paper-making flourish from the heavily-timbered land, and the beautiful Tasmanian blackwood is used for cabinet making, an aid to Tasmania's steadily increasing economy.

Tasmania attracts the tourists, but Australia has a rather small tourist industry. Even though the air net-works allow easy travel, accommodation is often poor.

## OPPORTUNITIES

The Commonwealth is an ancient land, but it is a young country in terms of the white man's occupation. It has endless opportunities for the brave and the resourceful, and for those with the scientific knowledge that can be applied to everyday jobs. Many parts are still wild and lonely, but they are just that much more exciting and challenging.

# THE UNIVERSAL LANGUAGE OF SMILES

*Photos :]* [*Mondiale*

The language of smiles is universal. Even though we may not understand her speech, we can share in the pleasure of the Scandinavian maiden on the left, who has removed an ugly witch-mask to display her own pleasant smile. The Indian girl, with her caste-mark on her brow, smiles in a more coy manner.

*Photos :]* [*Mondiale*

A Mongolian princess of Pekin shows her amusement in a restrained smile. The shy grin on the right comes from a Nepalese peasant woman, with large earrings and long bead necklaces. She carries a child in a cloth slung on her back.

*Photos :]*          *[Mondiale*

This cheerful Eskimo woman has something to smile about. It is a matter for great rejoicing when a narwhal is caught, for the skin and blubber are considered great delicacies. The Masai belle, below, from Tanganyika, gives a coy smile, secure in the attractions of herself and her elaborate ornaments. The Lapp woman on the right gives her version of a pleasant smile.

[Mondiale

This interesting relic of old sea-faring days was dug out of a burial mound in Norway, and carefully restored. It has been preserved in Oslo Museum, and shows how the Vikings built their ships many hundreds of years ago.

# CAVALCADE OF SHIPS

### by J. E. PRYDE-HUGHES, F.R.G.S.

THE progress of shipbuilding can be traced from very early times. The primitive vessels still in use to-day in many parts of the world provide notions of how the earliest men came to take to the water, and gradually gained confidence to venture out to sea and travel from place to place in floating craft. It is most likely that the simple human beings of prehistoric times watched trees floating down the rivers and wondered. Their curiosity aroused, they straddled floating tree trunks, and after finding that the larger logs would carry them safely, they soon discovered that they could guide these logs, perhaps with branches or rough stakes, and later, formed paddles. The more intelligent then realised that two or more logs bound together gave greater support, and after the success of the raft, came the idea of shaping the logs to give better control, and so followed by stages the hollowing of tree trunks and eventually some kind of dug-out canoe. These craft now could be utilised for the carrying of heavy goods

from place to place ; adventurous fellows put to sea and learned something of sailing. So they came to other inhabited places. There was a diffusion of knowledge, and the art of building water craft spread widely as the years passed by. That at a later date anyway there was a wide spread of shipbuilding and other knowledge is suggested by the fact that early Scandinavian vessels have parallel constructions in the islands of Oceania.

In the year 1896 parts of a very early vessel were recovered from the peat bog of Halsnö in Norway, and proved to be of great interest expecially when compared with the remains of Viking ships found in various places in Norway and Denmark. For instance the planking of a Danish ship of the third century consisted of several strakes overlapping at the lower edges and held by iron nails. The frames when placed in position with cleats were lashed tightly by means of bast cords. This principle was employed in the building of larger ships for many centuries afterwards.

The Halsnö boat was clearly more primitive, for no nails were used and the planking was sewn together with fibres. Now this type of boat of inserted frames lashed to cleats is not to be found anywhere in Europe outside Scandinavia, in fact, is seen nowhere else until one reaches Oceania, where in the different islands craft of a similar style of construction are found. At the same time, in these islands other parallels with things of ancient Scandinavia exist, such as, for instance, the burial of a chieftain with his ship. It is thought by some, therefore, that these ideas have a common origin and that thousands of years ago they spread to the Pacific, perhaps by way of the Siberian coast, the Kuriles and the Japanese islands, to the south.

In the islands from the Malay Peninsula to the Pacific and south to New Zealand there are to be seen numerous different kinds of craft, from very simple rafts and outrigger canoes to elaborate vessels with decks which remind one of the heyday of the Polynesian sea rovers who spread over the Pacific and linked up islands thousands of miles apart. Though there is no definite record of the great migrations it has been possible to trace some of the long voyages of these adventurers, who amongst other hazardous ocean pioneerings probably risked the unknown Indian Ocean and reached Madagascar. Similarities of boat construction in widely different places help to piece up the story of these early voyagers, in the same way that peculiar primitive craft help in the task of tracing the evolution of the canoe, boat and ship. In places where timber was unobtainable or scarce it is probable that early man utilised other buoyant materials like inflated hides, as is still being done in parts of India, or skins stretched over light wicker work, like the craft used on the river Tsangpo in Tibet, and the coracles used by the ancient Britons and still made and employed in parts of Ireland and on the rivers and estuaries of Wales. Then, too, in South America, off the coast of Chile and Peru, and on Lake Titicaca in the Andes, there is a very special light wood called Balsa, which is so light that a few baulks bound together, or bundles of rush-like material worked up into the shape of a boat, served for fishing and for the transport of heavy loads. These "Balsas" in their primitive form are still used to-day as they were centuries back, and an interesting modern sidelight is that

*Photos :]*          *[Mondiale*

Many peculiar kinds of craft can still be seen in different parts of the world. On the left, native women of Papua, New Guinea, are coasting over the warm waters in an outrigger canoe. The tub on the right, which is a copy of the coracles used by the ancient Britons, is at home on the River Towy, in Wales.

[Mondiale

In bygone days, when the Romans saw themselves as conquerors of the world, they set forth to war in a fleet of picturesque-looking ships, such as are seen above. It was not so picturesque, however, below deck, where the galley-slaves were forced to ply their oars ceaselessly, taking the place of the machinery which would one day drive ships and men speedily and comfortably across the ocean.

this light wood has proved of the greatest usefulness in airplane construction and was an important item in the building of the famous "Mosquito" fighter-bomber.

Egyptian pictures of three thousand years before the birth of Christ reveal well-developed boats, and by the time of Noah, about 2800 years B.C., shipbuilding had become an important trade. As to Noah's ship in which he and his family and a cargo of all sorts of animals lived out the Great Flood, we learn from the Bible—translating the cubit, the unit of measurement, to 18 inches—that it was about 450 feet long, 75 feet wide and 45 feet deep. So it was a large vessel even by to-day's standards.

The earliest records obtained from Egyptian tombs and monuments give one to suppose that the first ships of any definite style were seen in the delta of the Nile. That is, of course, in reference particularly to that part of the world. In those calm waters experiments could safely be made, and as the art of shipbuilding progressed no doubt the sailors ventured far-

ther afield, most likely into the Mediterranean. The fact that quite large vessels were used on the Nile and beyond the shores of Egypt gives rise also to the theory that the huge blocks of stone utilised in the erection of monuments like the Sphinx and the Pyramids were brought here by water, for the materials are not of local origin, and water transport would have been much easier than overland. Some sculptured works support this theory and in some tombs, supposed to be of Libyan origin and dating from between 5000 and 6000 years B.C., pottery has been brought to light with representations of ships on it. One of the representations depicts a big vessel of fifty-eight paddles on each side and with cabins and a deck structure. This ship was steered evidently by three paddles on either side.

As we come down the ages records of sailing from Egypt to the Holy Land, and into the Red Sea are available and in vessels which had progressed from paddles to banks of oars and even sail. Steadily sailors adventured farther

[*Mondiale*

A mock battle is in progress in one of the shrouded islands of the Solomons. The invading natives, landing in their long canoe, are met with fierce resistance from the " enemy," who, nevertheless, admire the fine craft which has brought their neighbours so swiftly across the water. This glorified canoe has the combined advantages of speed and space, and is so light that it can be easily manipulated.

afield in improved ships, and merchants traded in the Indian Ocean, while naval fighting craft were also evolved. Phœnicians, Greeks and Romans took up the course, and long before the opening of the Christian Era, the Phœnicians, who were a great seafaring people, came to Britain and even sailed round Africa.

In the years 980-947 B.C., when Hiram was king, Tyre was the greatest trading city in the Mediterranean, and Phœnician ships sailed far and wide collecting great riches from India, Africa and the west. In the third year of his reign, Hiram commissioned a travelled merchant, named Mago, to prepare ships for voyaging to the colony of Tarshish (Spain) to collect silver. Two war galleys were built especially to protect the convoy. They were each nearly 120 feet long and 30 feet broad and each had twenty-five oars. Being of shallow draft they could be propelled swiftly through the water. The freight ships were plumper. They had three decks and were armoured with plates of copper. The upper deck and the horsehead in the prow were painted red and lapis lazuli blue. In the bows platforms of Lebanon cedar were placed for the look-out man.

Mago's fleet sailed west, touching at various places and fighting off pirates and enemies like the Etruscans. To damp the ardour of Greek competitors in these waters the Phœnician seafarers spread terrible stories of Scylla and

[*Mondiale*

The Romans rule the waves. Here is a reconstructed glimpse of a Roman war-vessel, returning victorious after one of its sea-battles. In those days the Mediterranean " belonged " to the Roman Empire, and any rival ship was swept off the waters, or sent to the bottom of the sea.

Charybdis, the horrible Cyclops and fearsome creatures with faces on their chests and flying serpents. With the same purpose the Etruscans built their barques in the form of fantastic monsters; but they failed to frighten or stop the Phœnicians, who eventually came to Tarshish and loaded silver into two galleys which returned to Tyre eighteen months later.

Meanwhile the adventurous Mago put out to the west with his remaining vessels, past the columns of Melkart at the straits of Gibraltar,

island which the sailors named the "Happy Isle." It was in the Canaries. Instead of returning, the Phœnicians continued southward, turned the Cape and reached the Red Sea by way of the east coast of Africa. Egyptian officials at the Canal of Pharao (Straits of Suez) had doubts of the vessel and her wretched men, but Mago and the remains of his crew reached Tyre at last with riches in tin, amber, sandalwood and gold dust.

It was about this time that navies began to

The Northmen of old sailed the seas in "dragon" ships, similar to the model seen above, which was excavated at Riga. The largest of these picturesque ships was about 25 yards long, with a beam of about 12 to 18 yards.

which to all in those days marked the end of the land of the north world. Eventually he came to an island which he reported was one large tin-mine. Mago wrote that the inhabitants of this island voyaged along the coast in boats made of hides sewn together and called themselves "Britons." (He could not know that the wild people of these islands would come to be as daring seafarers as were the Phœnicians three thousand years ago.)

Mago went farther still, to the mouth of the Elbe and met Finnish, Slav and Germanic barbarians, and on returning from the north reached Cadiz again. Here a storm drove his ships out to sea and the next land seen was an

fight at sea and in the Mediterranean piratical craft lay in wait to attack the increasing merchant shipping plying between the countries on the shores of that sea. At the opening of our era the Roman war galleys had gained control of the sea and practically cleared the Mediterranean of enemies. The galley type of ship with a single bank of oars had by this time proved itself as more efficient and easier to handle than the ships with two or three tiers of oars. These vessels of three banks of oars were known as triremes, and this name came to be applied generally to the warship. But it was the galley that persisted and continued to be built right down to the sixteenth century.

Sail, however, was of increasing importance, and shipbuilding, not restricted to the Mediterranean shores, developed in Northern Europe and in the busy ports of our islands too.

Before the coming of the Scandinavian freebooters and subsequent invasions from the Baltic countries, the Britons were backward as a seafaring folk, and in this respect it was the Veneti, a people of Brittany, who for a long while commanded the sea trade of the English Channel. Their vessels were staunchly built of beams with flat bottoms and driven by sails of dressed hides. The British vessels of those days were less sturdy and frequently little better than the coracles still used by fishermen in the quieter waters of Wales. This craft, whether used on inland waters or along the sea shore, was just a wicker framework over which hides and skins were tightly stretched, making them buoyant and watertight.

THE Saxons, when they settled in England, showed great interest in shipbuilding, especially as sea-going craft became essential in the defence of these shores against the marauding Danes and other groups of invaders from the northern waters. King Alfred the Great, who took the matter up seriously and with energy, might be considered as the founder of the British Navy, for before he built his fleet there had been nothing in the nature of groups of warlike vessels seen in these islands. By the tenth century the British Navy was well established, and the vessels maintained numbered thousands. They were sailing ships built of planks with strong keel which extended beyond the body of the vessel to form a ram. Like most early ships they were highly ornamented both bow and stern, and carried a deck structure.

About this time the Norsemen were sailing and ravaging along the whole western seaboard of Europe, and even pushed into the Mediterranean. They discovered Iceland and Greenland, and there is evidence that they even sailed to and settled in what are now known as the New England States of America. The ships in which they undertook such venturesome voyages were really clinker-built boats about 80 feet in length and 16 to 17 feet in breadth. From gunwale to keel the depth would be about 6 feet. The planking of the frames was held in place by iron rivets. The Norse ship was propelled by oars and sails, and so sea-

worthy was it, so excellent its design for strength and buoyancy, that it has not been excelled even unto this day.

In the Middle Ages shipping developed in all directions. During the fifteenth century, the age of discoveries, the Portuguese and the Spaniards especially drove their sailing vessels over all the seas. Their seamen opened the way to America and round the Cape of Good Hope to India and the Spice Islands of the Java Sea. British adventurers took up the challenge and there was a great race to build larger and more enduring ships. The British developed a man-o'-war with four masts and strong forecastle, with many guns and cabin accommodation for passengers, officers and crew, and in such vessels, and lighter and faster ships, they undertook daring voyages of discovery and contested the mastery of the Atlantic with the powerful Spanish fleets.

The *Santa Maria*, in which Columbus sailed to America, was a ship 128 feet long and 26 feet broad, and it had a displacement of 233 tons, a fairly large vessel for those days, but a mere decorated cockleshell by modern comparisons. She had three masts and bowsprit. A little later the famous *Great Harry*, built at Erith and launched apparently in June, 1514, was of over 1000 tons.

The most important maritime event of the late sixteenth century was the sailing of the Spanish Armada to suppress Britain. It was a fleet of 132 vessels of which the largest was a galleon of about 1250 tons, mounting thirty guns, and with a crew of eighty sailors and 344 soldiers. In those days soldiers were put on board the ships to do the fighting. The largest British ship to oppose the Armada was the *Triumph*, of about 1000 tons and with forty-two guns.

From these days the big sailing ships, with tiers of guns peeping from their sides, grew in size and form and continued on much the same lines right down to the last century. With the opening up of the Far East came the demand for speed, and this introduced the famous clippers, British and American, which raced under enormous spreads of canvas to and from the farthest ports with trade goods and cargoes of tea, spices and other commodities.

These clippers challenged each other on the wide oceans and competition in design and structure and in accomplishment between the

*[Mondiale*

Many strange materials go to make up the cavalcade of ships. Here, in the South Seas, we find banana stem lashed together to make a primitive craft on which a native is happily paddling on the placid waters.

*[Mondiale*

Another discovery shows a Portuguese caravel, with its stately masts, and an interior view below decks. It is interesting to reconstruct the lives of those who sailed on board, and to consider the perils they encountered on the uncharted seas, when seafaring was a daring adventure.

[*Mondiale*

A graceful schooner, ignoring the more powerful antics of a passer-by, sails calmly across the untroubled water. Seen from the air, it seems like a small bird with its wings spread in flight.

Americans and the British, and indeed amongst home traders became intense. Many of the sporting runs by these graceful vessels home from the Far East after weeks at sea are now history. The people on the Channel shores watched for and cheered the clippers as they fought their way urgently to the great port of London.

The introduction of steam propulsion and the use of iron in construction gave a new direction to ship design and character. This change of power and material enabled the building of larger and faster vessels, and size and power steadily increased until the monster liners and battleships of up to 50,000 tons were reached. Whether ships will continue to increase in size beyond this is questionable. Other considerations must now be taken into account with the utilisation of a new element, the air, and in the service of long-distance travel there is promise of huge air-liners carrying passengers, mail and merchandise all over the world at undreamt of speeds, and completely eclipsing surface vessels in rapid transit.

[*Mondiale*

A Queen of the Seas—S.S. *Queen Mary* in New York Harbour. Although nowadays the *Queen Mary* is no longer the last word in shipbuilding and design, she is still a fine example of a modern luxury liner.

# AN EASY WAY OF EARNING A LIVING

[*Mondiale*

You could take this photograph for 3d. ! In Lapland the Lapps rely on the reindeer for food, drink, clothing, and for transport. The old Lapp in the photograph has, however, found another use for his beast. He poses for photographs to the visitors, charging 3d. a time !

[Mondiale

In Sweden, " Starboys," representing the wise men from the East, go from door to door singing their songs. The Star King is in the centre, and the one dressed in black and carrying the money-bag, represents Judas.

# CHRISTMAS AT HOME AND ABROAD

## *by* ISOBEL KNIGHT

CONTRARY to popular belief many of our Christmas customs have come down to us from days long before the birth of Christ. The hanging of the mistletoe and the burning of the yule log are ceremonies passed on to us by our pagan ancestors. Druids regarded the mistletoe as a sacred plant. They believed that it would cure any manner of disease and if carried on the body, would render a person safe from witchcraft.

One very beautiful Scandinavian legend regarding the mistletoe has been handed down the centuries. Here it is.

Once upon a time long ago, when the world was young and the gods walked the earth, Balder the god of poetry dreamed that he was going to die. He told the dream to his mother, Friga the goddess of love. Friga called the world of nature and received a promise that her son would not be harmed by anything which grew on the earth or under the earth.

Strong in the faith of this promise Balder went forth into battle where spear and arrow left him unscathed. One day Loake his enemy was walking through the wood when his eye alighted on a sprig of mistletoe climbing up an oak tree.

"Anything growing on the earth or under the earth," said Loake to himself. " But this is neither. The mistletoe grows on a tree." Hastily pulling some of the plant, he wrapped it round the tip of his arrow, and went to the blind god Heda. By means of subtlety and craft Loake persuaded Heda to shoot the arrow. It pierced Balder and he fell dead.

Everything in heaven and earth wept for the young god, but he was miraculously restored to life by his mother Friga the goddess of love, whose tears turned into the little berries of the mistletoe.

"Neither on the earth or under the earth," so that, legend says, is why the mistletoe must always be hung up high.

The burning of the yule log, a custom which, up till the present century was celebrated with much pomp and ceremony, comes to us from our far distant Scandinavian ancestors, who at their annual feast of Juul, kindled huge bonfires in honour of the god Thor.

In our great-great-grandfathers' day passersby doffed their caps as the great yule log, sometimes the whole length of a tree, was dragged along the road to the house. There were all manner of superstitions about the yule log. It was considered very bad luck if a person with a squint came into the hall where the log was burning; most unlucky of all was the presence of a flat-footed woman.

On Christmas Eve the fun and merriment began, and many queer games were played. One favourite was to suspend a scone dipped in treacle from a beam in the ceiling, each person taking it in turn to jump and try to secure a bite.

Most popular of all old-time Christmas sports, was snapdragon. A large handful of raisins was placed in the bottom of a broad shallow dish. Brandy was then poured over the fruit and it was set alight. All lights in the room were extinguished. The game was an exciting one, as each partaker had in turn to step forward, and putting his hand into the flames, try to secure a raisin.

When this entertainment palled there was the mirthful game of questions and answers to fall back on. Here one person was selected as "the commander" and the rest of the company were his "subjects." The commander could command any subject to answer any question he liked to put. If a subject could or would not answer he had to submit to having his face blackened as a penalty.

Mumming occupied an important place in the Christmas festivities of olden days. Wardrobes were ransacked, boys dressed up as girls, and girls as boys, and together a band of young people would go from house to house in the district sometimes giving a display of dancing, sometimes presenting a pageant or a play. During the reign of Henry the Eighth the wearing of masks was forbidden, the king ordering that all persons found wearing one be arrested as vagabonds and put in prison for three months. The reason given was that murderers and robbers were taking advantage of the disguise and mixing with the merrymakers.

Christmas dinners were stupendous affairs and sometimes included as many as sixteen principal dishes with as many other "small asides." Most important of all was the Boar's Head. The whole company rose to their feet as the head with sprigs of rosemary peeping from out its ears, and a lemon in its mouth, was carried in state on a silver dish by the chief cook.

Other dishes included swan, heron, partridge, peacock, larks, venison, boiled capon, roasted goose, and perhaps roasted pig. Among these the peacock was second only to the boar's head, and the preparation it required before coming to table was no mean task. The skin was first carefully stripped off leaving the feathers intact. The bird was then roasted and when cool slipped into its skin and feathers again, and sewed together. The beak was covered with gold leaf, and a piece of cotton soaked in spirit and set alight placed in its mouth. This noble dish was considered such a speciality that no servant was permitted to serve it, instead, women guests picked for their birth and beauty bore it to the festive table.

In our own land as well as in many continental countries many of the old Yuletide customs have died out. In all Christian countries, however, the Christmas season is regarded as the festival of children and the time of goodwill towards man.

In Poland Christmas Eve is a fast day and feasting does not begin until the first star twinkles in the sky. Then all members of the family gather together, a few straws in remembrance of the Stable at Bethlehem are scattered on the floor, and father, mother, and the children sit down to supper. One chair is left vacant, in case, perchance, the Christ Child should want to join the feast. Small round wafers which have been blessed by the priest and stamped with the imprint of a sacred figure are distributed to all members of the household, who break these between them, wishing each other joy and happiness.

Children in Poland know Father Christmas as "The Star Man." Often he is the priest in disguise. He examines them in the catechism and rewards them with presents.

On Christmas Eve in Holland the young men dress up in fancy costume and meet in the village square. There they sing a Christmas hymn and choose one of their company as Star Bearer. The Star Bearer is given a big star-shaped lantern and this he carries at the head of the procession which, singing Christmas carols, wends its way in and out of the streets.

Animals and birds are remembered at Christmas time in Finland. All the cows and horses get a special Yuletide dinner, and every householder places a sheaf of corn on his roof that even the birds may have a share in the joyful festivities. On Christmas Day everyone rises before dawn and makes their way to church, from the windows of which shine a galaxy of candles.

Turkey, plum pudding and mince pies are probably your favourite Christmas fare, but if your home was in Brittany, cod would be the special dish at your feast. If you were an Italian girl or boy, eels would be the most popular dish, and if you lived in certain parts of Germany you would be almost certain to be served with herring salad. Pig is the principal Christmas dish eaten in Roumania.

The original Father Christmas was St. Nicholas who was Bishop of Myra in Lycia at the beginning of the fourth century after Christ. St. Nicholas had plenty money and a kind heart. He was never happier than when he was helping poor people and giving them presents. The Bishop was a very humble man,

however, and he did not want to have his generosity talked about, so all his gifts came as surprises. Sometimes a poor family would find a gift on their doorstep, or a gold coin would make a miraculous appearance on the floor after St. Nicholas had visited a house where the people were in want.

At last one day someone caught the Bishop in the act of leaving one of his anonymous gifts and the secret was out. His kindness and goodness have not been forgotten, and although it is sixteen hundred years since the fine old man died, to-day when someone receives a gift from an unknown person, St. Nicholas or his more modern name of Father Christmas, gets the credit for it.

Norwegian children believe that Father Christmas employs an assistant to help him. They call him by the fascinating name of Kris Kringle. Kris Kringle's work is to drive the fairy-built sledge packed with presents over the snow-capped roofs.

In many European countries St. Nicholas is regarded as the special patron saint of boys, and St. Lucy as the guardian of girls, so in Switzerland Father Christmas is supposed to arrive accompanied by his wife Lucy, who

[*Mondiale*

The people of Denmark make Christmas a gay and colourful festival, with lighted Christmas-trees in every window, and presents for all. Here is a " public " tree in Copenhagen, sparkling and twinkling for all to see.

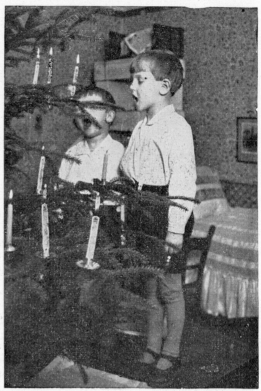

*Photos:]*                                                        *[Mondiale*

Christmas is the children's festival, and all over the world they enjoy it in much the same way, though their customs may be different. The Dutch child on the left is in ecstasy over her Christmas tree ; while the Czecho-slovakian children on the right sing carols round theirs.

distributes the gifts to the girls, while Father Christmas attends to the boys.

On Christmas Eve, French and German children leave their wooden shoes at the side of the fireplace. When they waken in the morning these are filled with presents, but every child is warned that if she or he has been misbehaving, a piece of wood instead of a toy will be found in the shoe.

In Spain and Italy the giving and receiving of gifts is sometimes put off till Epiphany. In this way the people commemorate the story of the Wise Men, who led by the Star in the East travelled to the Manger to give gifts to the Baby Jesus.

A curious custom is prevalent in Spain. Here the children do not leave their shoes by the hearth on Christmas Eve; they put them outside the window that "the Wise Men" may fill them with gifts on their return journey from the Manger at Bethlehem.

No one knows the origin of the Christmas Tree, but there is no country in Christendom where it does not make its annual appearance bedecked with gifts and shimmering with fairy lights. There are many legends connected with the Christmas Tree, but perhaps one of the most beautiful comes from Northern Europe.

One Christmas Eve a peasant and his family were sitting round the fire. The snow was lying deep and the wind was whistling through the trees. Just as they were thinking of retiring for the night a knock came to the door. The father got up from his seat, and opened it. On the threshold stood a little boy, poorly clad and blue with cold.

"Come in, my child," said the kindly peasant and he brought him to the fire.

"You must have some food," said his wife, and she gave him a steaming plate of soup.

The children shyly clustered round the little stranger.

"You can have my bed," whispered the youngest.

So they rolled the little stranger boy in warm blankets and tucked him up snugly in bed.

On Christmas morning the family were wakened by the sound of sweet singing, and when they looked at the little stranger to whom they had given hospitality, lo and behold, they found he was no ordinary little boy, but the Christ Child himself.

In great amazement they watched him as he opened the door, walked a little way down the snow-covered path and came back carrying the branch of a fir tree.

"See, I will plant this tree for you," he said, and moving away the snow, he pressed the branch into the earth.

"You have given me your gifts, now I will give you mine. This tree will not be like other trees. Henceforth it will bear its fruit at Christmas time. It will have something for you all, and it will be your Christmas Tree."

When the Christ Child had spoken these words he walked out into the snow and disappeared from view. The peasant and his family gazed at the branch of fir tree with wonder in their eyes, then they looked at the carpet of snow surrounding their cottage. Its white velvet smoothness was undisturbed. The Christ Child had left no footprints.

[Ibüsz

The children of the country districts of Hungary perform a Bethlehem play at Christmas, dressing up for the occasion and going solemnly through their parts. Note the miniature representation of the Manger at Bethlehem, held by the lady on the right.

# THE VEILED MEN OF THE SAHARA

"YES," I thought, "I really might be on the moon," as I gazed at the weird peaks of naked rock spread out in front of me. My feet were in the hot sand; the sun burned down fiercely; when I put my hand on a boulder beside me, it was almost too hot to touch. There was no speck of greenness, only sand, littered stones, and mountain crags.

I turned round with relief and looked at the oasis of Tamanrasset behind me, where the green of palm and tamarisk showed inside its high walls. Tamanrasset is encircled by these Hoggar Mountains; and they are in the very middle of the mighty Sahara desert.

The Sahara is so vast that you could fit about seventy Englands into it. It stretches across the whole of North Africa, from the great bulge of the west coast to the banks of the Nile. You could journey for a thousand miles southwards from the Mediterranean, and still not be out of it. You will have often seen in films and photographs a string of camels swinging across the golden sands. This may have given you the impression that the desert is all sand. That is very far from being true. There are, for instance, many immense plains of sharp black stones. You can stand in the middle of one of these and see nothing but blackness from horizon to horizon. And there are these mountains of the Hoggar Plateau, the greatest of which is more than twice as high as Ben Nevis, the loftiest peak in Britain.

There are hardly any continuous ridges or ranges. Most of the peaks stand alone, rising sheer from the desert. Some are shaped like huge pyramids; some like turrets, square boxes, or spear-heads. One or two rise in an array of towers like vast cathedrals. And the sunlight picks out their wonderful colouring, from pink and mauve to jet black.

## WHERE THE FOREIGN LEGION FOUGHT GRIM BATTLES

Before the middle of last century no white man had seen the Hoggar. Then a few daring explorers wandered into the Sahara and brought back tales of these fantastic mountains. The French, from their headquarters in Morocco and Algeria, started their slow conquest of the desert, when men of the Foreign Legion fought their grim battles with savage tribesmen. At last, just after the opening of this century, the French gained control over the Hoggar after a fierce and lonely battle. They built a fort at Tamanrasset which they named Fort Laperrine, after one of their greatest commanders.

To-day, Tamanrasset has a sandy street lined by the neat mud-houses of French officers and officials. The steel aerial-masts of the fort tower up into the sun-filled sky, and supply lorries come lurching and bumping through its gates. These have sometimes come all the way from Algiers, over a thousand miles of the great desert track which the French call the *Ligne de Hoggar*. You may live in comfort within the walls of Tamanrasset, but it is a tiny speck of civilisation in an unchanging wilderness.

Did anyone live from choice in such a desolate waste before the French came? Yes, the Hoggar was, and is, the home of a mysterious people called the Tuaregs, or, as the Arabs describe them, "The People of the Veil."

That morning, as I stood watching the mountains, a Tuareg man strode past me. He was tall and erect, and clad from head to foot in dark robes. Over the lower part of his face was a mask, or veil, so that his steady brown eyes met mine through a narrow slit between veil and head-dress. On his chest swung a bunch of leather charms. He took no notice of me, but went on his way towards the mountains with long, raking strides. He reminded me of a race-horse as he moved across the desert.

## THE TERROR OF THE SAHARA

The Tuaregs were once the terror of the Sahara. Imagine these strange, masked warriors on their magnificent white camels descending on some encampment or oasis in the first light of dawn! They fought savagely with sword and spear, killing some, and carrying off other unfortunate victims to be sold as slaves. These men despised anyone who cultivated the land or who was a merchant. It was the Tuaregs who first blazed the caravan trails across the desert, and dug the

A picture of the moon?  No, these are the grim, naked peaks of the Hoggar Plateau.

Primitive agriculture. The Tuaregs use small hand sickles when harvesting their meagre crops.

wells along them. They would carry goods and slaves for other people, but they produced nothing themselves.

As I watched the proud figure of the Tuareg fade into the distance, I wondered why his face was thus hidden. Amongst many peoples it is the custom for the women to be veiled. The faces of the Tuareg women are uncovered; it is only the men who wear the veil.

I do not think the Tuaregs themselves know the origin of it. To keep the sand and dust from blowing into their nostrils, some writers have said. In that case, why do not both men and women wear veils? As a disguise when raiding? Why, then, do the men still wear their veils when they are alone with their own families? Even when they are eating, they raise only the lower edge and slip the food into their mouths. It is a strict rule that the man keeps his face always covered, and no one has yet discovered the real reason.

A French officer at the fort had told me the camp of the *Amenokal*, or king, of the Hoggar Tuaregs was in the mountains, somewhere in the direction in which the man ahead of me was going. I decided to try to find it; it was still quite early in the day. The *Amenokal* had

a little palace in Tamanrasset, but he was nearly always to be found in one of the desert encampments. One thing, in particular, I wanted to discover. How do the Tuaregs live now?

When the French finally conquered them, all slave-trading was stopped, of course. They also stamped out the fierce inter-tribal fighting, in which so many innocent people were butchered. To the Tuaregs, who had been warriors for centuries, this was like saying to an agricultural people, " You must stop cultivating the land; you must find something else to do." Had the Tuaregs found anything else?

I soon found out one answer. In about two miles, after trudging over ground like a pebbly seashore, I came upon a small group of them. I have said they have for centuries despised the man who grows his own food. This particular little colony had evidently revised their opinions, for they had built themselves mudhuts, and had sown small patches of wheat. It was only about a foot high, but it had fine fat heads, though it seemed to be growing in pure sand. The patches were about eight feet square, and they were surrounded by a trench

A nobleman of the Tuareg tribe, once the terror of the Sahara

He admired and loved the wandering Tuaregs, and he did more than any other man to win the friendship of the people of the desert for France.

His dwelling was little more than a cave; his water a tiny spring, so small that if a gazelle had sipped it, he had to wait a whole hour before he could have a drink himself. He was a very brave man, for he lived alone among people who at that time bitterly hated their conquerors. His life ended when he was assassinated in Tamanrasset during the first World War, when the desert tribes became restless and almost forced the French out of the Sahara.

At last I came to a sandy valley, entirely surrounded by silent, cindery-looking mountains. There were little greyish-green plants growing, and some tufts of withered grass. A herd of camels was grazing, and in the midst of it was a square hut made of dry, bundled reeds. This was the king's shelter; near it were low tents of stretched skins in which his servants and household lived.

It was disappointing to find the *Amenokal* was not there, but his wife and two young sons clad in white robes saluted me gravely. She

into which water could be poured. The veiled men were harvesting the wheat; pulling it up in handfuls, and drying it in small bundles.

## A SHOWER OF RAIN IN THE YEAR

You have to dig for water in the Hoggar. I asked another Frenchman how often it rained. He said: " Oh, I believe we had a shower last year! " If you know where to dig, say in a dry river-bed, you may find water twenty feet down; or you may sink a hundred-and-fifty-foot shaft before you strike it.

The Tuaregs pointed vaguely in the direction of the mountains when I asked, " *Amenokal?* " I went on. The sun was directly overhead; when I looked down, my shadow was a dark puddle round my shoes. It was March, and the real summer heat had not yet closed in on the desert. There was a strong breeze, but it was far hotter and more glaring than any summer day in Britain.

In the far recesses of the mountains I was just entering, a famous French priest and missionary built himself a lonely shelter some fifty years ago. His name was Père de Foucauld.

The white-robed sons of the *Amenokal*, or King, are not yet fully veiled.

was a tall, beautiful woman; her face was unveiled, but she would not let me take her photograph. The sand floor of the hut was covered with a bright carpet. There was an old enamel saucepan, and two small teapots in a corner. Under a skin shelter I saw some saddles and panniers, an old gun, and spears and swords. There was no food anywhere. These few simple things were all the possessions of the king of this proud race! Except for his stately white camels pulling at their dry grazing.

## LIVING ONLY FOR THEIR CAMELS

I now realised fully that something I had been told by a man who knows a great deal about the Tuaregs was exactly true. The Tuareg lives only for his camels; they are his pride and the centre of his whole life. Try to picture this life. Here was this lonely encampment. It could stay in this valley only as long as there was grazing for the camels.

When the stunted plants were finished, the Tuaregs would have to roam through the mountains till they found some more. Again the shelters would go up; and again they would have to continue their wanderings when the camels had eaten all they could find. So year after year they would move through this stern and silent land, living almost solely on the rich milk of their camels. Perhaps some of the elders remembered the thrills and perils of their warrior days; but most of them had known only this monotonous journey from pasture to pasture. So far, they seem to be happy.

We could not speak to each other, but I gave them some tea and sugar, and we sat on the carpet smiling and talking slowly by signs. Their language is strange; Père de Foucauld was the first man to succeed in writing it down. Many of the letters are in the form of a pattern of dots, believed to be copied from the star-groups which the Tuaregs see as they lie

How would you like to read this writing? This is how the Tuareg reads his Scriptures. It is from the Book of Ruth, translated by the Scottish Bible Society.

The dark-veiled figure on the left is the *Amenokal*, or King of the Tuaregs. Like the rest of his tribe, he lives simply, his most prized possessions being his camels.

under the glittering night sky of the desert.

## A COLD PLACE WITH A BURNING SUN

The Hoggar has been called a cold place with a burning sun. It must indeed have been bitterly cold curled on the floor of that flimsy hut, with the night wind hissing through the reed walls. There is sometimes a difference of fifty degrees between the day and night temperature. It is like being plunged into a frosty winter night after bathing and sun-bathing on a hot summer day—and having no snug house to go into! That is what the Tuaregs have to endure; but they have never known anything different.

Dusk was approaching, and I had to depart. I hurried along the valley, and at the first corner picked up my landmarks—the slender aerial-masts of Fort Laperrine silhouetted against the glowing sunset. There was the new world! Turning round, I took a last long look at the old. Small fires flickered in the dusk, for the wind already had a chilly edge to it. A few figures moved round the skin tents, and the two white-robed boys were looking after me and waving.

Would they still be wandering through these mountains when they were as old as the *Amenokal*, their father? Or might they have forged some new, more productive life for themselves in this harsh and cruel land?

# MOTHER OF PARLIAMENTS

EVERY country has to have a government. There are three main reasons for this. The first is that there must be someone to keep order among the people. A country is not just a large area of land; it is a large group of persons living together in that area. Our British islands with their population of over forty million form one of the important countries of the world. Those forty million are separate individuals, men, women, boys and girls, each with his or her own wants and wishes. But it would hardly do for all of them to act in every way just as they pleased. We all know that you must not steal, or cheat or cause danger to others. When food is short, we must each take our fair rations. We must not use counterfeit money. If you are a shopkeeper you must not give short weight. To prevent people from doing these things laws are made. Laws are also made about other things. There are laws about getting married, laws which say who shall have a person's property after he is dead, laws saying how masters shall deal with their servants, laws which require children to go to school. All these laws are made so that the people of this country shall behave properly towards each other.

The second reason for having a government is that someone must make arrangements for the defence of our country. We have to have an army, navy and air force to ward off enemy attacks. It is also necessary to organise our country so that our mines, factories and fields produce the goods we need. It may also be necessary, in times of emergency and difficulty, to make sure that our workpeople are all employed making the things we need most.

## PUBLIC SERVICES

The third reason is that, in a modern civilised country like ours, there have to be proper roads, schools, hospitals, water supply and drainage, electricity, parks, libraries and many other advantages which uncivilised countries and savage races do not have. These things are known as public services.

To see to all these things—public order, national defence and public services—there has to be a government to decide what to do and to see that it is done. Courts of justice are provided to decide when any laws have been broken. Police forces are maintained to see that law-breakers are caught and punished.

We have two sorts of government—national government and local government. National government deals with the country as a whole, makes the laws, organises the country's defence, and sees to its general welfare. Our national government is provided by the Queen and the two Houses of Parliament, the House of Lords and the House of Commons, assisted by a body of officials known as the Civil Service. Local government deals with the management of small areas—towns, counties and parishes. There are borough councils and urban district councils for towns, county councils for counties, rural district councils for the country parts, and parish councils for the villages. These councils are mainly concerned with the public services, the roads, schools, sanitation, and things of that sort. The councils can also make local laws for their own areas, known as by-laws.

## OUR MODE OF GOVERNMENT NOT INVENTED

This short statement of what government is for, and the two forms it takes—national and local—does not give any idea of who the people are who actually do the work of government, or how they do it. What are the Houses of Parliament? Why are there two Houses? What part does the Queen play in all this? Who are the members of these various local councils, and how do they get there, and when they are there, what is it they can do?

In other words—How are we governed? And why are we governed in the way we are? These are big questions, and there is much that can be said about them.

We should be very proud of our British form of government. Our Parliament has been called the " Mother of Parliaments " because the parliaments of other countries are modelled on ours in many ways. Our Parliament is the oldest.

An ancient lock-up where, in former times, offenders were detained to await transportation to court or jail.

The stocks: A popular form of chastisement in the Middle Ages. Evil-doers were secured by the ankles and made to endure public scorn and abuse.

A thousand years ago, an area surrounding Ripon Minster, called "The Sacred Mile," provided sanctuary from the King's men to refugees from the law.

Ducking-stool: A punishment to which gossips and nagging wives were subjected. They were secured in the chair, then dipped into the village pond.

Our form of government was not just invented. It took many hundreds of years to grow up to what it is to-day. To understand why it is like it is, and how it works, we must go back deep into the past. It makes quite a long story, and one which every boy and girl should know and love.

## BRITONS—ROMANS—SAXONS

Most books about English history begin with Julius Caesar and the ancient Britons.

Our story need not begin so far back. Although Britain was a Roman province for four hundred years, little remains of the Roman occupation. The names of one or two places which have the ending " caster " (such as Lancaster), or " chester " (such as Winchester), show they were once Roman camps. Here and there are a few ruins. Some of our roads follow old Roman roads. But the Romans have left no mark on our form of government.

After the Romans, came wave after wave of

Angles, Jutes, Saxons and Danes; invaders from Northern Europe. What we call England became, then, a cluster of small kingdoms. These invaders have left only small traces in our present way of government, and these traces are mostly in the names we use for local government purposes. " Shire " for instance, as in Yorkshire or Devonshire, was the Anglo-Saxon word for a large district corresponding roughly to a modern county, and the sheriff, an officer who still exists, was once a " shire-reeve," an important official with great authority in the shire. The by-laws which

The Domesday Book was an extraordinary record which William the Conqueror had compiled. It gave an extensive survey of land tenure and population in the 11th century.

An entry in the famous Domesday Book, so-called because it was an exact record of every man's wealth against which there was no appeal.

are made by local councils to-day get their name from " by " the Danish word for town (as in Derby, Whitby), and so are " town"-laws.

## NORMAN FEUDAL TIMES

During the centuries before the Norman Conquest in 1066, there gradually grew up in England, and in many other parts of Europe, the system of government which we call the feudal system. The idea was that the King owned all the land in the country. Some of it he kept for himself, but most of it he divided

into " fiefs " or big estates which he allowed the great lords, dukes, earls and barons, to have. In return, these great lords swore loyalty to the King and promised to bring soldiers, money and weapons to help him in war. Each great lord in turn divided up his estate into smaller fiefs called " manors." These manors were given to lesser lords, each of whom promised to bring his share of armed men, money and supplies in time of war. The lesser lord, or lord of the manor, would in his turn give small pieces of the manor to farmers, in return for promises to serve as soldiers, or to send a shield, horse or spear as might be desired. Some tenants might pay a rent in money to their lord instead of giving military help in this way. When William the Conqueror

The ancient village of Corfe from the ruins of the Norman Castle, symbol of feudal and royal power and demolished in Cromwell's time.

became King he strengthened the feudal system throughout the whole country.

The feudal system was not just a way of getting together an army. It was a system of government as well. It affected almost everything that people did in those early times. Each manor was rather like a separate village, with its own craftsmen making clothes and other goods for village needs. Some of the villagers were freemen; others—most of them —were serfs or villeins compelled to work on the lord's land. They were allowed to share in the common land of the village but were not allowed to leave the manor.

## THE KING'S OFFICER

The lord of the manor was the ruler of the village. He and his bailiff called together the meeting of freemen known as the " court " to decide matters of village government—the division of crops and land, repair of the roads and so on. The King interfered only in certain limited ways. He (or his judges) had the right of trying and punishing crimes like murder and theft, for example. The King's officer, the sheriff, travelled round to see to the military arrangements, and to make sure that the great feudal lords did not become so strong and wealthy as to be dangerous rivals to the king.

The Church was also a great landowner, with its own pyramid of feudal lords who held fiefs though they were not compelled to serve as soldiers for them. To the ordinary serf it made little difference whether his manor belonged to a baron or to an abbot or bishop of the Church.

There were few towns in feudal England. These were centres for making and exchanging goods of better quality than those made in the villages. In them were gathered free craftsmen and apprentices who had left the farming life of the country to make a living by their trade. As the townspeople became wealthy they were able to buy from the lord of the manor the right to hold their own courts and to be exempt from work on the lord's estate. In the same way they would buy from the King a " charter." This was a big, imposing document in which the King gave the town various special privileges. One privilege often given was that the town was only to be taxed if the townspeople agreed to it. Another was that the town should have its own corporation, with a council elected by the townspeople to manage the town's business, run the local court, and generally to act for the inhabitants as the lord and his officers did for a country manor.

## THE GREAT CHARTER

Without an understanding of the feudal system it is impossible to understand Magna Charta, the Great Charter, which King John gave to the barons, and which has had a great effect on our system of government.

# CITIES OF REFUGE

THE RIGHT OF SANCTUARY originated in the very early days of the history of civilisation. The pre-Christian Jews had their cities of refuge, and the Egyptians, Greeks, and Romans had resorts where the wrongdoer, and such as were hunted on account of imaginary crimes, or vengeance, could, in the days of primitive justice, claim protection from pursuers. The sanctuaries were sacred, and in Britain were rarely violated. An exception was Tewkesbury Church in Gloucestershire, where, after the battle of the Bloody Meadow (War of the Roses), blood was spilt in the Sanctuary, with the result that the church was

The " Chair of Peace."

The Sanctuary Ring at Durham Cathedral.

closed for some months and had to be re-consecrated.

The church of Beverley, in Yorkshire, was most renowned, the treasured privilege being conferred upon it by King Athelstan, who also granted the right to York, Ripon and Hexham. But Beverley and Hexham only still preserve the Frid-stol, or "Chair of Peace," gaining which the criminal, or hunted man, no matter what his crime, or how horrible, short of treason, was safe, even from the vengeance of the king.

As a result of abuses, but chiefly on account of the Church harbouring wrongdoers unlawfully, Parliament curtailed the privilege of sanctuary, and finally abolished it. Yet the humanitarian custom was responsible for preventing a great deal of bloodshed.

London, of course, and other towns had places of refuge, and all the relics of these still existing are now carefully preserved as national monuments. " Ye Olde Staire Inn," at Alfriston, Sussex, was an instance of a non-religious building possessing the privilege, sanctuary right having been conferred upon it by the Abbot of Battle Abbey.

# BRITAIN'S OLDEST MAN

"OLD PARR" died in 1653, aged 152 years, and he is generally acknowledged to be Britain's oldest man. But there is an obelisk in Bolton-on-Swale, near Richmond, Yorkshire, to the memory of an older man, Henry Jenkins, whose life, testified to by an investigating committee, lasted 169 years. The church register states that he died in 1670, having lived through the reigns of Henry VII, Henry VIII, Edward VI, Mary, Elizabeth, James I and Charles I, and the Commonwealth (1649-1660). The committee discovered that Jenkins claimed to have delivered a horse-load of arrows at Northallerton, when he was twelve years of age; he remembered the dissolution of the monasteries, and also the assembly of the English forces before Flodden Field; he visited the Abbot of Fountains Abbey, where he was entertained with food and beer. The cottage in Ellerton-on-Swale where Jenkins lived is still occupied. An inscription on the obelisk states that he was " a person of obscure birth, but of a life truly memorable . ."

An old-fashioned couple in an old world cottage in Henry Jenkins' village.

To these children the Amazon is not merely a name in a geography book. It is the mighty river that flows past their homes and on whose banks they play every day. Life for them is full of colour and sunshine.

# THE WORLD'S WONDER RIVER

## by HAROLD J. SHEPSTONE, F.R.G.S.

THERE is certainly no waterway crowded with such a startling array of animal, bird and insect life as the Amazon, the colossus of the world's great rivers. Its banks are lined with tropical forests that stretch a thousand miles and more in every direction, much of which is largely unexplored, and here dwell not only a host of weird and wonderful creatures but many Indian tribes. Thus to the naturalist and lover of wild life the Amazon makes a unique appeal.

It is, in fact, the most alluring of all rivers, standing in a class by itself. You cannot compare the Amazon to the Nile, the Ganges, St. Lawrence or the Mississippi, for it has an intriguing spell of its own. Rising in the Andes, in Peru, it flows right across the South American Continent, virtually following the course of the Equator for a distance of 4700 miles. With its innumerable tributaries, many of which are over a thousand miles in length, it drains an area two-thirds the size of Europe. So great is the outflow of this single river system that it tints the deep blue of the ocean a tawny yellow colour two hundred miles

from its mouth. It discharges six million tons of fresh water into the ocean every minute and is responsible for one-tenth of the fresh water of the globe.

To-day modern liners ascend the river as far as Manaos, a most fascinating city, dumped down in the very heart of the primeval forest, lying just over a thousand miles from the river's mouth. From this point, river steamers can be taken to Iquitos, another 1400 miles farther up the river in Peruvian territory. Although the Amazon is associated with Brazil it flows for over a thousand miles through Peru. Just before the war an interesting air service was established from Iquitos, over the jungle and waterways to San Ramon on the upper reaches of the river, and from here one proceeds by motor and train to Lima, the picturesque capital of Peru. The air journey from Iquitos to San Ramon occupies about four hours. By boat and canoe it takes ten days owing to the many twists of the river.

Although the Amazon is nearly two hundred miles broad at its mouth it is so crowded with forest-clad islands seemingly overburdened

95

with vegetation that its immense width is not noticed. Here stands Para, the gateway to the Amazon. Like all towns on the Amazon it is surrounded on all sides, save by the river, by dense jungle. It was at Para that the great naturalist Bates lived and wrote his famous treatise on the insect life of this region. He found over 14,700 insects, of which 8000 were unknown. But many more have been discovered since his day.

Para, too, has grown from a miserable, fever-stricken settlement into a busy, bustling city with many fine public buildings, electric light, trams and modern hotels. With its quaint native bazaars and curio shops displaying painted calabashes, snake and jaguar skins, alligator teeth and curious pottery and its busy market-place, where you meet natives of every shade, from the coffee-coloured Indian to the coal-black Barbadian negress, Para is decidedly cosmopolitan in character.

One of its sights is the Bosque—an area of tropical vegetation, which was left untouched when the thick growth was cleared from the river-bank to make room for the expansion of the city, and which serves as the traveller's introduction to the Amazon jungle. Here the frail assia mingles with the slender bamboo, and countless varieties of palms, tall grasses, bright flowers, and buttressed forest-giants form a riot of vegetation. In the middle of this jungle is a large pond wherein dwells an old specimen of that strange fresh-water mammal, the manatee, or cowfish, so named because its face is not unlike that of a cow

There is also a cave here wherein nest hundreds of bats, including that dreaded species, the vampire. The collection of native bird life seen in the zoological gardens is not only large but very representative. To the ornithologist the Amazon to-day is a veritable paradise. Over forty species of parrots and at least fourteen species of macaws have been recorded, in addition to which there are parakeets, the toucan with its huge bill, the spoonbill, heron and crane.

But the river calls, and boarding our steamer we proceed through the Narrows, and for the next hundred miles or so steam along deep but narrow winding water lanes between large and small islands clothed to the water's edge in tropical vegetation. So narrow is the channel in places that the sides of the boat are swept by the branches of the overhanging trees. When the main channel is reached you are amazed to learn that it is some twenty miles across. But it is so crowded with large and small islands, and steamers have to pass so close to them, that you fail to recognise the immense width of the stream.

As the mouth of the Tapajos is approached, no mean tributary of the main stream, seeing it is a thousand miles in length, you notice a curious phenomenon. The yellow water is streaked with patches of green. A peculiarity of the river is the varying hue of its waters. Some of the streams are jet black, others are almost white, green, or deep olive hue; due, it is said, to the colour of the soil over which they flow. Yet the water is actually as clear as

[*H. J. Shepstone*

Para, the gateway to the Amazon, is a cosmopolitan city, combining a mixture of old and new. Natives of every shade mingle at the bazaars and the docks, where modern buildings tower in the background.

[H. J. Shepstone

Here is an aerial view of part of the wonderful Amazon, the very name of which conjures up romantic visions of exotic scenery, of the colourful people who live on its banks, and of the variety of strange animals and insects which make their homes in and around this majestic river.

[H. J. Shepstone

Liners ascend the Amazon as far as Manaos, a city dumped down, as it seems, in the very heart of the primeval forest. From this point, river steamers can travel another 1400 miles up the river to Iquitos, among scenery which seems to rival Fairyland in its beauty and variety.

Photos:] One of the most unusual fish found in the waters of the Amazon is the man-eating piranha, shown above. [H. J. Shepstone
Although no larger than a herring, it will attack anyone who ventures near it. The howling monkey on the right, with its long tail which it uses as a fifth arm, is one of the many inhabitants of the Amazon forest.

crystal. Dip it up and place it in a bottle to settle and it quickly loses its colour or sediment.

It was down the Tapajos that Sir Henry Wickham penetrated just over sixty years ago, secured some rubber seeds from the wild trees and smuggled them out of the country. They were brought to Kew Gardens where they took root, and it was from these seeds that the great rubber plantations of Ceylon and Malay States had their birth. When Sir Henry was collecting his seeds and filling little bags with soil the Brazilians pointed to their foreheads and said he was mad. It was one of the means, however, of calling attention to the untold wealth of the illimitable forests that line the banks of this mighty stream.

During the day gorgeous butterflies, with a spread of wing as large as your open hand, flit about the boat, and birds of brilliant plumage disturbed from their afternoon siesta, cross the river, or fly along the forest-clad banks. At night immense moths of delicate colouring are attracted by the lights of the boat, and very weird are the harsh cries of the howling monkeys in the nearby forests. The noise this animal is capable of making is almost beyond

belief. It begins with a roar, changes to a growl, and after that to a deep groan. An interesting feature of the monkey-life of the Amazon forests is that with very few exceptions they possess prehensile or grasping tails that are as useful as a fifth arm or hand.

There are cries of "Boto!" This is a kind of river dolphin, which is very fond of following large and small craft. They love to gambol on the surface of the water like porpoises, and have a habit of gasping and snorting violently. But the Amazon is rightly famed for the variety of its fish, which include species found nowhere else. There is a lake near Manaos, the January, which is said to contain 1500 varieties of fish; yet all the rivers of Europe combined cannot boast of more than about 250 species. A very extraordinary fish found in certain of the Amazon streams is the man-eating piranha. Although not much larger than a common shad or herring, it does not hesitate to attack anyone venturing into the water. In the London Zoo there is a specimen of the paraque, or electric eel, which came from this region. Merely to touch it is to get a shock which you cannot shake off for hours.

*[H. J. Shepstone*
The alligator shown above is another of the numerous creatures who make the Amazon their home. Many fierce battles are waged on the banks and in the water, and the law of " the survival of the fittest " reigns supreme.

A line of white and pink bungalows denotes the little township of Itacotiara, the centre of the Brazilian nut industry, all the nuts being gathered from wild trees. So the voyage continues, the interest never flagging, until Manaos, a picturesque modern city on the left bank of the Rio Negro, is reached. Rio Negro means black river, and its glossy black waters form a striking contrast to the yellow current of the main stream. Manaos forms an ideal jumping-off place for excursions into the forests or launch trips to the creeks to see that wonderful aquatic plant, the Victoria Regina. With their upturned edges its leaves look rather like huge floating trays, but are so buoyant that a child can stand upon them.

Not far from Manaos are the Taruma Falls. Part of the journey is made in boats and thence through dense forests, where you have to thread your way behind native guides. It is a fascinating experience, for you are in a new world where man appears puny. In the forest dwell many weird and wonderful creatures, though you may only catch a glimpse of a few of them—the tapir, the big cats, such as the black leopard, jaguar, ocelot and puma. Then away up in the tree-tops, hidden from the sight of man, beautiful birds build their nests and rear their young, and here the sloth spends his upside-down life. In the lagoons the crocodile may be seen and in the swamps dwell the anaconda and boa-constrictor, often referred to as water-snakes as they spend so much of their time in the stream. Above all, there is the continuous noise, for the Amazonian forest never sleeps, day or night. There is the shrill chirrup of the cicada fly accompanied by the drone and buzz of a myriad other insects.

*[H. J. Shepstone*
The manatee also finds house-room in the Amazon, where it feeds on water-plants. It is a slow, clumsy creature quite harmless but often persecuted for the sake of its oil, skin and flesh. The Indians, however, hold it in superstitious reverence and allow it to live in peace.

To many of us pineapples are a rare luxury, to be tasted seldom and to be seen only in small quantities in a shop window. Here, however, they are growing as profusely as potatoes ; and many of us would enjoy helping with such a harvest.

# PINEAPPLE ISLAND

### *by* J. E. PRYDE-HUGHES, F.R.G.S.

WHEN Captain John Kidwell first settled near Honolulu in 1882, he was able to indulge his hobby of plant growing. The pineapple was then a wild, small, woody fruit whose flavour was acid, though pleasing. Kidwell, discovering the wild pineapples growing near Honolulu, saw an opportunity for horticultural experiment. He attempted to improve the size, texture and flavour of the fruit by cultivation, but the only result was a larger pineapple whose flavour and texture were apparently unchanged. Then Kidwell thought of the Jamaica pineapple, known as the Smooth Cayenne, a variety of higher quality. He imported and planted a thousand slips. The dry red sandy soil of the islands proved a tonic for this particular variety. The fruit developed magnificently and produced a large, lusciously sweet, smooth-surfaced pineapple of fine texture.

His success encouraged Kidwell to open a cannery on the island of Oahu in 1892. The venture met with little success, and soon Kidwell sold his plantations and cannery and retired from business.

Kidwell's experiment was an important development in the history of pineapple in Hawaii, but the real foundation of the industry was not laid until 1901, when a young Bostonian named James D. Dole, who was crofting a small tract of sixty acres in an outlying district of Honolulu, organised the Hawaiian Pineapple Co., Ltd.

Since then the importance of pineapple as a Hawaiian industry has increased tremendously. To-day more than fifteen or twenty million cases of pineapple and pineapple juice are shipped each year to all parts of the world, but mainly to the mainland of the United States.

The Hawaiian Pineapple Company now has approximately 25,000 acres of land under cultivation on the islands of Oahu and Lanai, the latter a smaller island of the Hawaiian group with an area of 140 square miles.

Until 1922 Lanai's characteristics were chiefly cactus plants and scattered herds of cattle.

[*Mondiale*

A new crop being planted in Pineapple Island.   Strips of paper, about 3 feet wide, are laid down to discourage the growth of weeds and to conserve heat and moisture within the soil.   Holes are punched through the paper, and each cutting of the pineapple is then carefully planted out by hand.

[*Mondiale*

In twelve or fifteen months after planting, clusters of flower-buds, very similar to the pineapple fruit,  appear in the heart of the plant.   These gradually wither and die, and in another four or five months the mature pineapples are ready for picking.   Here is a very prolific and luscious-looking crop.

Tractors soon tore out the cacti, highways were built and a harbour hewn out of the rocky coast. A city, complete with schools, bank, stores, and a hospital, was built to house the people who would later work in the pineapple fields, and now approximately fifteen thousand acres of Lanai's cultivable area are producing pineapples that are shipped to the company's plant at Oahu. Lanai has become one of the principal sources of the world's finest pineapple.

Although the dry, red, sandy soil, temperate climate, and tropical sunshine combine to make Oahu and Lanai a natural paradise for pineapple, the Hawaiian product would never have reached its present perfection if scientific methods had not been rigorously applied.

The field must be carefully cleared with tractor ploughs, sub-soilers and harrows, to put the soil in the proper condition for planting. Strips of mulch paper in rows three feet wide are then laid upon the freshly ploughed earth. This paper, similar to tar roofing paper, discourages the growth of weeds and conserves moisture and heat within the soil, thereby giving the young plants every opportunity for sturdy growth.

Planting, which takes place as soon as the mulch paper is laid, is a hand process. Holes are punched in double rows through the paper and into the soil with a tool which resembles an automobile tyre iron and is known as a planting iron. In each of these holes a slip is planted.

Fertiliser in the form of an iron sulphate solution is sprayed over the leaves, and ammonium sulphate is applied by hand to the lower leaves. An oil spray is used to protect the plants against insects.

The pineapple is not grown from seed, but from slips of which there are three distinct varieties: one, called the "crown" which grows from the top of the fruit; another, called the "slip" which grows in clusters at the base of the fruit; and a third, known as a "sucker" which grows from the central stalk of the plant at the base of the leaves. The seeds of Hawaiian pineapple are rare and are used only for experimentation in developing different varieties of fruit. A few weeks after the slips have been planted they take root and send out new leaves. In twelve to fifteen months after planting, a reddish, conical cluster of flower buds appears in the heart of the plant. This cluster is very similar to the pineapple fruit in appearance,

[*Mondiale*

Remarkable machines, known as " Ginacas," are employed to speed the pineapple harvest on its way. These "robots" remove the crown from the fruit, peel and core them at the rate of 85 to 108 pineapples a minute.

*[Mondiale*

Girls, wearing rubber gloves and spotless caps and aprons, inspect and trim the golden cylinders of fruit at long tables, after which the pineapples are sprayed and passed to a machine which cuts them into uniform slices, ready for grading and packing.

but has tiny blue or violet flowers projecting from its sides. At any one time no more than four or five of these flowers appear. They are ephemeral, lasting only a few hours. Nearly a month is required for all the flowers to open.

As the flowers gradually wither and die, the flower head develops into a fruit, the crown grows larger, and in four or five more months a mature pineapple—sun-ripened and luscious —is ready for picking. The mature pineapple plant stands about waist high. A period ranging from fourteen to twenty-six months elapses from the time of planting until the first crop is ready to harvest. The pineapple plant is unique in that it produces but one fruit, known as the plant crop, at the time of the first picking.

After the plant crop is harvested the other shoots, called "suckers," develop. Field employees remove all but two of these suckers. Each sucker left on the plant produces one pineapple after twelve months—fruit which is known as the first ratoon or second crop. Subsequently a second ratoon or third crop is developed similarly. Usually it is the final crop harvested before the land is ploughed for rest and replanting.

Although pineapple picking continues throughout the year, the heaviest months are June, July and August. In Hawaii, the pineapple is never picked until its sugar content and flavour mark it as perfectly ripe.

In harvesting the crop, pickers walk between the rows of plants and pluck the fruit by breaking it from the stem. Behind the pickers a machine known as a field fruit carrier is driven down the rows under its own power, followed by two men who lift the picked pineapples from the tops of the plants on which they have been laid and place them on elevators at the rear of the carrier. These elevators carry the pineapple upwards to buzz-saws, which lop off the leafy crowns from the fruit. Men standing on the platform of the carriers then load the fruit in boxes, which are later transferred to lorries and to the packing plant.

In the cannery the fruit is first fed into

103

remarkable machines known as "Ginacas," which remove the shells and cores and leave the fruit in cylindrical form cut to the proper diameter to fit within the cans. Ginaca machines handle from eighty-five to one hundred and eight pineapples a minute.

The golden cylinders of fruit are conveyed from the Ginaca machines to long tables where girls, all wearing rubber gloves and spotless caps and aprons, carefully inspect the pine-apple and do whatever trimming is necessary. The trimmed fruit then passes through a spray of artesian water, and next passes through a machine which cuts it into uniform slices with one stroke of an assembly of knives. Fol-lowing this operation, the fruit is conveyed to packing tables where girls, with gloved hands, make the proper selections as to grades and fill the cans.

After leaving the packing tables, the filled but still unsealed cans of fruit are subjected to a vacuumising treatment. In the first step a machine known as a pre-vacuumiser collapses all air cells in the fruit, assuring uniform tex-ture and colour in the product.

The cans are then conveyed to adjoining syruping machines. Like the pre-vacuumisers, these are revolving devices on which each can is automatically raised against a valve. The pressure opens the valve, allowing a uniform quantity of syrup to be discharged into the can. The valve automatically closes when the can is lowered as it leaves the machine. The syrup is made from pineapple juice and pure cane sugar.

After syruping, the cans pass into adjoining seaming machines, which attach covers to the cans in such a way as to produce, without use of solder, a hermetically sealed container. The hermetically closed cans of fruit pass from the vacuum seamers to cooking machines, through which they move continuously. In the process the fruit is completely sterilised. The cans next pass through a prolonged cold water spray in cooling machines, and are then stacked by an automatic operation on trays and removed to the cooling room, where they remain for at least twenty-four hours.

Dole pineapple juice is extracted from the same choice portions of fruit which might otherwise be used for the sliced product. After the can is filled with juice, it is subjected to the vacuum packing, sterilising, and cooking process just described. The so-called waste material, consisting of pineapple shells, ends, and trimmings is diverted to the by-products mill where it is put through a series of pro-cesses which produce pineapple bran, used for livestock feed.

[*Mondiale*

A rich harvest of pineapples, having left the island by barge, is now unloaded at the wharf in Honolulu. Before their journey is over, they may travel many thousands of miles, but will still preserve the " sunny " flavour of their island home.

Shakespeare's tomb in the chancel of the Parish Church, Stratford-on-Avon. It is seen to the right of the picture, with a bust statue of the famous poet over it.

# SHAKESPEARE, OUR GREATEST WRITER

### by H. A. TREBLE, M.A.

IT is strange that we know so little about the early life of the world's greatest poet and dramatist. The few known facts may be briefly stated at once.

William Shakespeare was born on April 23rd (St. George's Day), 1564, at Stratford-on-Avon in Warwickshire. His father, John Shakespeare, was a wool merchant and butcher. He was a highly successful man of business who, like many yeomen-farmers in various parts of England to-day, was able to make money in a variety of ways other than farming. He bought property, and in time reached the height of his ambition by becoming "High Bailiff"—or as we should call him nowadays, Mayor—of Stratford. Shakespeare's mother, Mary Arden, was the daughter of a well-to-do farmer and an heiress in a small way. She was of gentle birth. Without a doubt the dramatist owed a good deal of his own honesty and open nature to her—qualities that earned for him his distinction as "the gentle Shakespeare."

John Shakespeare, by reason of his being an Alderman, was entitled to have his son educated free of expense at the Grammar School at Stratford, and it is most probable that he took advantage of the privilege. Here the boy would be taught Latin and would learn to read some of the Latin authors in the original. Indeed it is unlikely that his instruction would go any further than this. Possibly Jacques's picture, in his famous "Seven Ages of Man" speech, gives us the youthful Shakespeare's own idea of school life:

"... the whining schoolboy with his satchel and shining morning face, creeping like snail unwillingly to school."

When an Elizabethan boy was idle or naughty in class he was punished in much the same way as an idle or naughty schoolboy often is to-day. The method used was a form of detention called "the black bile." When time came for work to cease and for children to go out to play, idlers were made to sit still and to repeat a written exercise they had neglected in class. An usher supervised this work, just as a prefect might do in a modern school. Next morning these exercises had to be handed in to the master "under pain of six jerks (i.e. strokes) to be surely paid." For more serious offences, three or four strokes with a birch—or "with a small red willow when birch cannot be had"—were inflicted. A few strong pupils held the victim down while this punishment was being inflicted. Children in Shakespeare's day were not unduly pampered. "To spare them in these cases is to hate them. To love them is to correct them betimes"—so we read in a book published in Shakespeare's own lifetime.

Close to Stratford was the Forest of Arden. All boys love woods and streams, and it is evident that Shakespeare did so. In the forest he romped at will and played the games of childhood that are common to boys of every generation. The late Sir Arthur Quiller-Couch tells us that once with a friend he tracked the Warwickshire Avon from its source to Tewkesbury. He hoped that by examining the scenes of Shakespeare's boyhood he would get a better understanding of the great poet. "Ultimately," he writes, "we came to the upper bridge of Stoneleigh Deer Park. A line of swinging deer-fences hung from the arches of the bridge, the river trailing through their bars. We, having permission, pushed cautiously through these. Beyond the barrier we worked to right and left, amazed. We had passed from a sluggish brook to a pleasant expanded river, flowing between wide lawns. . . . This was Arden, the forest of Arden, actually Stoneleigh-in-Arden, and Shakespeare's very Arden."

In the lovely woodland scenes of this forest (though he places it in French Flanders), Shakespeare gives as the real setting of his delightful comedy, *As You Like It*. Here, away from the painted pomp of the envious court, the little band of exiles "fleet the time carelessly as they did in the golden world." Here

"Their life, exempt from public haunts,
   Finds tongues in trees, books in running
      brooks,
   Sermons in stones, and good in every-
      thing."

Even Amiens, a Lord accustomed to the ceremony of court life, sings :

"Who doth ambition shun,
   And loves to live i' the sun,
   Seeking the food he eats,
   And pleas'd with what he gets,
Come hither, come hither, come hither:
      Here shall he see
      No enemy
But winter and rough weather."

Yes, even in his London days, Shakespeare's heart was in his home forest, in which, doubtless, like Sir John Falstaff, he had in his boyhood "pluck'd geese, played truant and whipp'd top."

It will be interesting and instructive to learn something about the conditions in which the people of Shakespeare's days lived. Houses had become much more refined and comfortable than they had been in Feudal times. "These English," said a Spaniard of some importance in Queen Mary's reign, "have their houses made of sticks and dirt." Some form of protection for them was still considered necessary. The castles of the powerful nobles had always

It was in this theatre, the " Globe," in Southwark, London, that Shakespeare's plays were first performed.

[J. Dixon-Scott

The story goes that, as a young man, Shakespeare was caught poaching in Charlcote Park, and brought before the owner, Sir Thomas Lucy. Shakespeare later wrote some scathing verses and hung them on the park gates.

been defended by a moat, the water for which was supplied by springs from neighbouring hills. In the early part of the sixteenth century this form of defence was used also for the houses of the gentry and even of the wealthier yeomen. Such houses were called "moated." Sometimes the house was completely surrounded by a moat, the bridge or bridges across which made the views much more picturesque.

Timber grew plentifully all over England, so it is not surprising to learn that timber, and oak especially, was much more used than stone for house-building. Here and there in the west-country towns stone was often used. The houses were "half-timbered," i.e. the walls and ceilings were largely composed of wood baulks, often of massive oak, filled in with plaster between the portions of wooden framework. Oak replaced the beaten mud and lime of which the floors had been made. In the centre of the houses there was a large general hall, frequently extending from floor to roof. In the midst of the hall was an open hearth, the smoke from which escaped through a hole

in the roof. The days of wall fireplaces came later in the sixteenth century. On both sides of the hall were rooms built in storeys. The top rooms were reached by a step-ladder. The lord of the manor and his family slept upstairs, the retainers on rushes strewn on the floor of the hall.

In the fifteenth and sixteenth centuries the internal arrangements of farm-houses and cottages were vastly improved. The aim was to increase comfort and privacy. In particular, in the hall and the parlour two wall fireplaces were added, back to back, with a common chimney of vast size. The open hearth in the centre of the hall was done away with. On the fireplaces were placed huge logs of wood, with smaller billets to help them to burn. In time the central hall was divided up into rooms in two storeys and the movable step-ladder was replaced by a fixed staircase. Thus gradually houses became more or less like the village houses of to-day.

Clusters of these half-timbered cottages and outlying farms made up the village of the sixteenth century. Judging from old cottages that still survive, the villages must have been very pleasing to the eye. Two interesting features deserve special notice—the "pound" and the "stocks." Straying cattle were placed in the pound—a walled enclosure maintained by the village authorities. Here they were kept until their owners redeemed them by payment of a fine. The man in charge of the pound was called the "pinder" or "pinner." Villagers guilty of bad behaviour were frequently punished by being "clapped in" the stocks. The offender's feet (and sometimes, too, his hands and head) were locked in holes in a heavy framework. Here he was kept for hours and sometimes for days, exposed to the insults and scorn of his neighbours passing by. Even to-day in some of our country villages and churches we can see relics of this instrument of punishment.

The homes of the wealthy lords were of great size and were most luxurious. In *Kenilworth* Sir Walter Scott describes Kenilworth Castle, the home of the Earl of Leicester, and Queen Elizabeth's visit. The splendour with which she was entertained would have

The "Stratford Shakespeare," a portrait which may be seen at his birthplace, Stratford-on-Avon.

ruined any but a very wealthy man.

In Elizabethan villages there was little provision for entertainment. From time to time they were visited by travelling shows, just as outlying villages to-day are occasionally visited by a circus. Strange animals and unnatural human beings formed part of these shows. Shakespeare hints at these strange exhibitions more than once. In *The Tempest*, for instance, he says that in England the monster Caliban, if put on show at a village fair, would make the fortune of the person exhibiting him. " Any strange beast there makes a man." The village people were attracted to these shows by a picture of the monster on view suspended on a pole outside the tent. So in *Macbeth* Macduff tells the defeated tyrant Macbeth that by refusing to fight he will "live to be the show and gaze o' the time. We'll have thee, as our rarer monsters are, painted upon a pole."

The England of Elizabeth's days is often referred to as "Merry England." Owing to the discovery of the riches of the Western hemisphere the world was becoming bigger and finer under the people's very eyes. When men are merry they sing and whistle. A famous historian says that in the time of great Queen Bess "music and song were the creation and inheritance of the whole people. The craftsman sang over his task, the pedlar sang on the footpath way, and the milkmaid could be heard 'singing blithe' behind the hedgerow." The best of all these songs are those to be found in Shakespeare's plays. These "lyrics," as they are called (because originally they were intended to be sung with an accompaniment on the "lyre"), are delightful in sound and lilt. Many of them were set to music by the greatest musicians of the time. Here, for example, is a verse of one of the most famous of Shakespeare's lyrics:

" Freeze, freeze, thou bitter sky,
   That dost not bite so nigh
     As benefits forgot.
   Though thou the waters warp,
   Thy sting is not so sharp
     As friend remember'd not.

Heigh-ho! sing, heigh-ho! unto the green
   holly:
Most friendship is feigning, most loving mere
   folly.
   Then heigho! the holly!
    This life is most jolly."

*[Crossland*

Shakespeare's birthplace in Stratford-on-Avon in Warwickshire. It was here that he spent his early days, going to the Grammar School and roaming about in the Forest of Arden.

*[J. Dixon-Scott*

Mary Arden, the mother of Shakespeare, lived in this picturesque cottage before she was married. In her day it was known as a Manor House. She was the daughter of a well-to-do farmer and was, according to these times, of "gentle birth." Through her influence, the poet earned the title of "the gentle Shakespeare," and owed much of his honesty and open nature to her example.

109

Photos :]
[J. Dixon-Scott

Welford-on-Avon, in Shakespeare's district, with its thatched roofs and narrow lanes, has changed very little since the poet's days. Below: a view of Anne Hathaway's cottage at Shottery, where Shakespeare as an ardent young man came to court her. Many sightseers come from far and near to admire this old dwelling.

*Photos:]*                                                             *[J. Dixon-Scott*

Here is an interior view of Anne Hathaway's cottage, showing above the old beamed kitchen, with its old dresser containing a shining array of platters, off which the young Shakespeare no doubt dined when he came to call on his sweetheart. Below is one of the bedrooms. The great four-poster, with its old carvings, takes up most of the space in the small room.

As a boy Shakespeare must have lived the kind of life that boys really love. Often enough he played truant from school in order to take part in countless adventures in the forest and fields near Stratford. Hence he was able to see Nature in all her moods, both fierce and tranquil. What he saw became real to him and made a lasting impression on him. When he describes what he had seen, his readers more than see it, they feel it too. He tells us, for instance, how he preferred the countryside to the towns:

"This shadowy desert, unfrequented woods,
  I better brook than flourishing peopled
     towns."

To us, in England, the weather is a joke, and often a serious joke. Indeed Americans refer to the British climate as a series of samples! Are we in England not able, some years, to have tea out of doors in February? And are we not glad, some years, to have a good fire in July? The summer of 1594 was a notoriously bad one and evidently impressed Shakespeare. This is how he describes it:

            "The spring, the summer,
The childing (=fruitful) autumn, angry
     winter, change
Their wonted liveries, and the mazed world,
By their increase (=different crops) now
     knows not which is which."

And here is the first half of what Shakespeare sang in praise of winter:

"When icicles hang by the wall,
  And Dick the shepherd blows his nail,
And Tom bears logs into the hall,
  And milk comes frozen home in pail,
When blood is nipp'd and ways be foul,
  Then nightly sings the staring owl,
       Tu-who!
Tu-whit, tu-who!—a merry note,
While greasy Joan doth keel the pot."

A beautiful picture of winter, surely. In our imagination we can easily see the shepherd blowing on his fingers to warm them, and the farm maid taking the scum off the top of what is cooking in the pot and making herself greasy in so doing.

We have talked about the sights and scenes of the Elizabethan countryside. We have seen how the country folk lived. Let us now say something about the popular beliefs of the time—part of what we call "folklore." Fairies are of no great importance to us nowadays, but with the people of the sixteenth century this was far from being so.

In *A Midsummer Night's Dream* Shakespeare introduces us to the whole court of the fairy world. Fairies were thought to be the tiniest of wee creatures. Like human beings they marry. Their king is Oberon, their queen Titania. The fairy King and Queen are jealous of each other, as mortals so often are. They quarrel so violently that their attendant elves

                    "for fear,
Creep into acorn-cups and hide them there."

To Queen Titania's dainty-limbed elves Shakespeare gives enchanting names—Peas-blossom, Cobweb, Moth and Mustard-seed. They frisk about and dance in the moonlight. Where they have been dancing they leave behind them the fairy rings—"green-sour ringlets"—which sheep will not eat.

Puck or Robin Goodfellow is the little sprite who is King Oberon's personal attendant. Like other elves he has magical powers. He can transform himself into other forms:

"Sometimes a horse I'll be, sometimes a
     hound,
  A hog, a headless bear, sometimes a fire."

He is the Warwickshire house-fairy, full of mischief. This "shrewd and knavish sprite" frightens the village maidens; but he often helps them in their household work, especially if they offer him some little reward for doing so.

In *The Tempest* Ariel and his fellow-spirits work under the command of the magician Prospero. In this respect he is unlike Puck who is free to run his course of mischief independent of all human control. Perhaps we may see in Prospero a prophetic picture of man in our own time who is so largely the master of the invisible powers of Nature. Man nowadays can fly, can sail under the sea, can put a girdle round the earth in much less time than even Ariel could. Perhaps we can see the coming of wireless when Ariel enters, invisible, and sings, "Come unto these yellow sands." Ferdinand is amazed when he hears the song but cannot see the singer. "Where should this music be? i' the air or the earth?" he asks. The brute Caliban tells Stephano:

"The isle is full of noises,
Sounds and sweet airs, that give delight and
hurt not."

We can almost, so it seems, hear a gramophone or a wireless set playing quietly in the background.

Somewhere about 1586 Shakespeare left Stratford and came to London. Why he left Stratford we do not know for certain. Tradition says that with some companions he had robbed a deer-park belonging to the local squire, Sir Thomas Lucy. He was prosecuted for poaching and in consequence was driven from his home. However this may be, Shakespeare lived in London for about twenty-five years. These were the years in which he learned much from the bustle and activities of the life around him. He came across sailors and travellers from far-distant lands and listened eagerly to all the tales they had to tell him. In particular, he became associated with the theatres and the players of the city. He touched up old plays and then turned to writing new ones of his own. He gathered a good deal of material for his plays from what he himself observed and heard in the noise and bustle of the streets. For example, highway robbers were in league with inn-servants. Then servants noted the arrival of travellers at the inn, and found out if they were carrying much money with them and which way they were travelling next day. They passed on to the highwaymen the information they collected, and a highway robbery was the result. This is precisely the kind of story that Shakespeare tells of the robbery of the Kentish yeoman of his 300 gold marks by Sir John Falstaff and his friends.

Shakespeare won for himself in London both wealth and honour. He became a member of

[J. Dixon-Scott

The Parish Church of St. John the Baptist at Aston Cantlow, where the father and mother of Shakespeare were married. His father, John Shakespeare, was an Alderman, and his mother was Mary Arden.

[*J. Dixon-Scott*

These Elizabethan houses, still standing in Mill Lane, Warwick, give a good idea of the kind of houses Shakespeare lived in and saw around him. Note the fine timbering and pleasing design, and the way in which the upper storey juts out over the lower one. In narrow streets it was sometimes possible to shake hands with your opposite neighbour from the bedroom windows.

a famous company of actors, and it was for this company that he wrote many of his later plays. But even in his days of prosperity in London he never forgot his native Stratford. We are told that he visited his "native country" once a year. The money he made from his plays he spent on buying property not only in London, but also in Stratford. In particular, he bought a house in Stratford called "New Place" to which he finally retired about 1610. Here he lived very quietly until his death on 23rd April, 1616.

We hope that what we have said about our great poet will do something to make our young readers like his plays and poems. These plays are not easy reading; but young people will probably understand a great deal of what they mean until, like the youthful reader of *Punch* who "understood the jokes quite well until they were explained to him," they begin to read *about* the plays instead of reading the plays themselves. Charles and Mary Lamb tell the story of a number of the plays in delightful and not too difficult prose. A preliminary reading of their version will be a very great help towards grasping more and more the fuller meaning of what the greatest poet of all time wrote.

*Photos:]* [*Two Cities Films, Ltd.*

These shots from Laurence Olivier's production of *Henry V.* show (above) a scene between Gower (Michael Shepley) and Fluellen (Esmond Knight); and (below) Pistol (Robert Newton) playing his part with great gusto at the Globe Theatre.

Photos :] [*Two Cities Films, Ltd.*

Above: The French Dukes fret under the indecisive action taken by the French King at Harry's approach. Below: The great battle scene, showing the French horses rearing and plunging under the impact of the English archer's withering fire.

The Shakespeare Memorial in Westminster Abbey. Note the words on the scroll, taken from *The Tempest*, Shakespeare's last play.

# THE SEAMAN'S FRIENDS

FROM the days when the Egyptians first ventured out over the waters of the Mediterranean, attempts have been made to warn sailors of dangerous rocks and shallows, which might bring disaster to their gallant little ships. For a long time the only warning signals which could be used were beacon-fires lighted on dangerous coasts. An attempt was made to build a lighthouse on the coast of Asia Minor seven hundred years before the birth of Christ, but the first one of which we have a definite record was built on the island of Pharos, near Alexandria, somewhere about the year 300 B.C.

This lighthouse was considered one of the seven wonders of the world, and served as the model for hundreds of others which were built on headlands or rocky islands during the following two thousand years. Not until the beginning of the nineteenth century was any great improvement made.

A modern lighthouse is a model of scientific and engineering skill. It is usually circular in shape, with walls ten to fourteen feet thick, and if it is built on a rocky coast it is so carefully dovetailed into the solid rock that it will withstand the most terrific storms. Inside the circular tower, one above the other, are the store rooms, the workrooms and the living apartments. At the very top is the great lantern with its clockwork mechanisms, and its huge lens, perhaps three times as tall as a man, its prisms and its reflectors, which not only magnify the light but collect the rays to form one tremendously powerful beam.

The light shown on the old towers was provided by wood or coal fires, and did not carry any great distance. The modern lantern may use either oil or acetylene gas or electricity. An electric arc lamp was first tried out in England in 1868, and was a tremendous improvement on anything previously used, but even this has now been superseded in many cases by a high-power incandescent lamp, the million candle-power light of which can be seen twenty miles away.

The lanterns are tremendously heavy but they work with the accuracy of the most perfect watch, sending their flashes out into the night in particular combinations, so that the sailor not only receives a warning but knows exactly which lighthouse he is passing.

But even the million candle-power light is useless when a thick fog descends over the sea. On these occasions, either sound rockets, fog-guns, sirens or diaphones are used, but the most important lighthouses are now able to send out wireless signals, which can give a ship a hundred miles away its exact position on the fog-shrouded ocean.

On some of the most lonely inhospitable shores of the world, there are unattended lighthouses. In some of these the lanterns work automatically by means of a wonderful piece of clockwork mechanism, others are controlled by electric cables connected to the coast.

Lightships are often used over dangerous banks and shoals. These lightships are fitted with powerful lanterns on steel masts and with apparatus for producing fog signals. If a fog-gun is used, explosive charges and their detonators are attached to an endless chain which carries them to the point where they are exploded by electricity. Many lightships are now equipped with wireless, but some of them are unattended and work automatically.

In river estuaries and other waterways, small floating vessels known as buoys are used as marks of navigation, and to give warning of dangers such as hidden wrecks, sandbanks and sunken rocks. These buoys, which are usually moored to huge blocks of cement, are generally made of steel plate, for they have to be extremely strong to withstand the fury of the waves, and the possibility of their being run down by passing ships.

Buoys are of various types. Light-buoys, as their name implies, carry a light, the source of which is a compressed gas; they are usually provided with a mechanism by means of which the light automatically dims and flashes at regular intervals. Bell-buoys are conical in shape, and are often employed in foggy waterways. Whistling buoys are particularly useful, for they carry both a light and a whistle.

Other types of buoys—the "can," the "spherical," the "pillar," the "truncated," carry no warning signal, but are used to indicate navigable channels in harbours and river mouths. "Wreck buoys" are distinguishable by their green stripes. All buoys have distinctive marks and lettering, and are entered on charts, so sailors are able to identify them, and to set their courses accordingly.

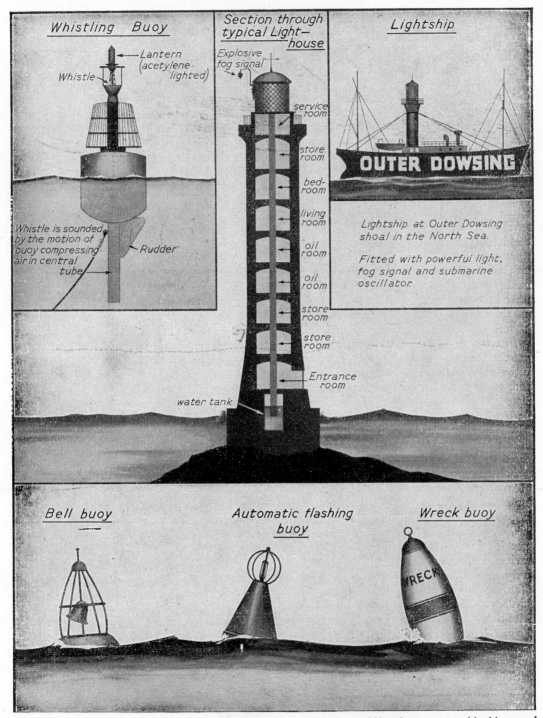

**Whistling Buoy**

Lantern (acetylene lighted)

Whistle

Whistle is sounded by the motion of buoy compressing air in central tube

Rudder

**Section through typical Light-house**

Explosive fog signal

service room

store room

bed-room

living room

oil room

oil room

store room

store room

Entrance room

water tank

**Lightship**

OUTER DOWSING

Lightship at Outer Dowsing shoal in the North Sea.

Fitted with powerful light, fog signal and submarine oscillator.

**Bell buoy**

**Automatic flashing buoy**

**Wreck buoy**

WRECK

The sailor has to face many dangers by night and by day. Fog blacks out his path, storms toss his ship to and fro, sunken rocks threaten to sink his vessel, and currents affect his course. There are no street signals or signposts in the sea, but their place is well filled by the lighthouses, lightships and buoys, diagrams of which are set out simply in the above picture with detailed explanations. These help to see the sailor through the hidden perils of the deep, and are the means of saving many lives.

# WAR AGAINST INSECT PESTS

*by* HAROLD J. SHEPSTONE, F.R.G.S.

A BATTLE that never ceases is that being waged by scientists in all parts of the civilised world against insect pests. Insects, grubs and fungi attack our crops, the fruit trees in the orchard, the trees in the forests, as well as our vegetables, doing untold damage. Though the contest has been going on for many years it is still no uncommon thing to hear that the apple crop has been a failure because of the codlin moth, or that cherries or plums will be scarce because the trees have been attacked by the saw-fly. In this instance it is not the fly that has done the harm, but the larva from the eggs it deposits. In like manner our carrot or onion crops are liable to suffer by attack from the carrot and onion fly, and the cabbage from the cabbage weevil.

Some idea of the colossal damage wrought by insects will be evidenced when it is stated that the Mexican cotton-boll weevil causes the cotton-growing states of America a loss of from twenty to thirty millions sterling annually ; the codlin moth costs fruit growers in the United States £2,400,000 a year; in Great Britain the ox warble fly destroys annually hides worth £400,000, and the frit fly is estimated to cause a loss of eight bushels of oats in each acre grown in an average year.

Not only do insects attack our crops, but they also affect our health. Man might be without such terrible scourges as African sleeping sickness, bubonic plague, yellow fever and malaria, were it not for certain insects, which act as carriers of disease. It has been shown conclusively that house-flies carry the germ of infantile enteritis and typhoid. Thousands of children under two years of age die in Great Britain alone every year from infantile diarrhœa.

Many of these insect pests are not natives of the country where they are to-day doing such terrible havoc. They have been brought in from other countries, carried perhaps in some new fruit or the root of a plant. Frequently they come alone, not in the company of their natural enemies. Finding conditions favourable, they multiply far more rapidly than in their country of origin. Such plagues as the European corn borer, the cotton-boll weevil and the San José scale have been imported into the United States, the woolly aphis and greenhouse white fly are supposed to have entered England from outside, while the dreaded grape-vine Phylloxera which, just before the war, threatened the wine industry of Southern Europe, is thought to have come from America.

Entomologists who are fighting these pests to-day first make a thorough study of the biology and ecology of the insects concerned. Not until this study has been made can an effective control be attempted. Strenuous efforts to acquire this knowledge for the British Empire are being made at the Rothamsted Experimental Station by eminent insecticide chemists; at the Farnham Royal Parasite Station where insect parasites and predators are specially studied; at the field laboratory of the Imperial College of Science at Slough; and at the Forest Products Research Laboratory at Princes Risborough, where forest insect pests are being studied. Medical entomological research is being done at the Liverpool and London School of Tropical Medicine. The co-ordination of these results and their practical application in the field throughout the British Empire are largely undertaken by the Imperial Bureau of Entomology.

Control measures vary considerably and are often long and costly. There is the physico-chemical control and the biological control to name the two most important. The first takes the form of dusting and spraying with various forms of poisons. For some years the hopfields of England have been successfully sprayed in order to keep the hop aphis within bounds. The most elaborate form of spraying is by aeroplane. Aeroplanes have been used for dusting large areas attacked by insect plagues with such poisons as paris green or sodium or calcium arseniate with some success in Louisiana, U.S.A., against the cotton-boll weevil and mosquito larva; in Germany against forest plagues; and in Northern Caucasia against the migratory locust. Aeroplanes have on one occasion been used in England against fruit tree pests near Sevenoaks, but in this country the use of the aeroplane is limited owing to the comparatively few large areas devoted to a single crop.

The biological control, in some respects the most interesting, consists in the employment of the natural enemies of the insect pest concerned. That enemy may be a bird or spider, but more generally it is an insect or parasite which in its native state feeds upon that particular pest. It means that you have to take that destroying insect to the infected area and in such numbers that its presence will have the desired effect. Care has to be taken to see that such insects will attack only the pest concerned and will not change their food.

Of these destroying insects employed by entomologists and agriculturists to-day the most remarkable is the ladybird beetle (coccinella). It was successfully used to control the cottony cushion scale in California, being introduced into that country from Australia. It is a pretty little beetle, generally of a brilliant red or yellow colour, with black, red, white or yellow spots. The form is nearly hemispherical, the under surface flat, and the legs short. When handled it emits a yellowish

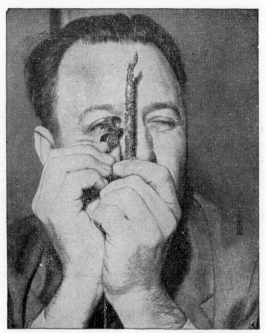

[H. J. Shepstone

The expert is here seen examining a potato sprout to determine the rate of growth of the disease known as black scale.

fluid, with a disagreeable smell. It lays its eggs in the leaves of plants close to the scale and it is the larva or grub that destroys the pest. There are many species of the insect, to be exact over 1500, and it is found all over Europe, including this country, and in certain parts of Africa and Asia.

To save the orange and lemon groves of Southern California, American experts are breeding ten million ladybird beetles and another twelve million parasites. They are being used in a mass attack upon the black scale and mealy bugs that infest thousands of trees among the citrus groves. It is the most daring and elaborate onslaught upon fruit pests ever undertaken. Scientists have struggled for twenty years to perfect an army of pest destroyers to kill first one insect, then another, which have threatened the Californian orange groves. Mealy bugs and an insect known as black scale cause untold damage. Black scale, which resembles a small blister, and mealy bugs extract the plant juices and generally sap a tree's vitality.

In the heart of the citrus district of Southern California stands a building known as the Rivera Insectary. Here ladybird beetles and the

[H. J. Shepstone

The superintendent of the insectary examines the ladybirds that are hatching out on material hung alongside the breeding boxes.

[*H. J. Shepstone*

The ladybirds have swarmed on to a screen that is well lit up. Then the trapper catches them in small gelatine capsules. As many as 57,000 ladybirds have been trapped in eight hours.

parasites who work with them are being bred in a wholesale way. One of these parasites was only recently discovered in South Africa. It is most effective in destroying black scale. To develop the host of beetles potatoes are first planted in hundreds of boxes. When the sprouts are about one foot high they are infested with mealy bugs by laying bags containing infested sprouts among the branches. Soon the young bugs crawl through the tightly woven mesh of the bag and attach themselves to the sprouts. When these bugs are one-third grown twenty-five beetles are placed in each box. These, feeding on the bugs, breed young which first attach themselves to burlap strips hung near the boxes and later, having emerged from their cases as adults, fly across the dark room to a screen covering the single window.

There they are collected, ten in each capsule. So rapidly do the insect trappers work, one has been known to scoop up 57,000 in eight hours. By means of an ingenious home-made slotted counter, the capsules are sacked in groups of one hundred.

Parasites resembling gnats which prey on

black scale are grown on pepper tree branches, oleander bushes and sprouts. The bug wizards release young parasites into tightly closed rooms where they attack and lay eggs within black scale growing on plants. Before the eggs hatch, the plants are transferred to collecting cages. When the young reach maturity an experienced bug-picker sucks them into test tubes, using an old vacuum cleaner for the purpose. Later these insects, each one-thirtieth inch long, are liberated among orange groves. Similarly do workmen scatter mealy bug parasites.

As already stated, ten million ladybird beetles are being bred, as well as seven million black scale parasites, and five million mealy bug parasites. As this army of 22,000,000 pest destroyers is ready they are thrown at the insect enemies swarming through the trees in a mass effort to beat back the attackers.

Thus nature herself balances the matter, and the useful insects live and thrive, and breed in the best circumstances. Their food will consist of the harmful insects that would, if left alone, create havoc among the fruits and vegetables, and thus man harnesses nature to assist him in increasing the world's food production.

[*H. J. Shepstone*

This machine checks off the capsules of ladybirds by hundreds. These are then ready for dispatch to the orange groves, where one will suffice for each tree.

[H. J. Shepstone

Here the distributor is tossing 10 ladybirds from a tube into an orange tree, where there is plenty of work for them to do. Many more tubes will be emptied over the trees, and the ladybirds, whose food is the greenfly and other pests, will immediately begin their good work of destruction, feeding on the harmful insects which would soon make havoc of the fruit if left alone.

For the first time in history, an invading army took its own harbour to the enemy-held shore. Here is one of the huge concrete caissons, weighing 7000 tons, being towed to the assembly point across 100 miles of channel. On reaching the Normandy shore, sea-cocks on each section were opened, and the caissons settled on the harbour bed.

# "MULBERRY," A MIRACLE OF WAR

## by J. E. PRYDE-HUGHES, F.R.G.S.

"**M**ULBERRY" sounds a queer name to give to one of the greatest achievements of war, and of technical capacity. But it served to shroud in secrecy an unprecedented effort on the part of engineers and workmen of Great Britain over a period of years, while vast preparations were being made for the invasion of Europe in 1944. It was only after the gigantic feat of the Normandy beach harbour was accomplished that the subject could be revealed to a wondering world.

For years this most imaginative work of war engineering occupied the attention of tens of thousands of scientists, engineers, technicians, soldiers, sailors and workmen, and as a result the extraordinary pre-fabricated harbour, known as "Mulberry" was in place, despite all obstacles—and they were many and nerve-racking—on time, and within twenty-four hours a quarter of a million of men were landed in France in the teeth of violent opposition. This opposition was supported by extensive fortifications which had been constructed

and strengthened over a period of four years.

By the twentieth day a million men went ashore, thanks to "Mulberry," and soon between two and three millions of American and British soldiers were fighting on the soil of France.

The problem of landing on the defended coast of Normandy was solved in the conception of constructing an immense system of pre-fabricated harbours piecemeal, with breakwaters and piers, and assembling them and disposing them to give large sheltered water areas at the site selected for the landing of the attacking forces. Tens of thousands of items had to be considered and dealt with, and the finished product was on a scale which dwarfed Dover harbour.

It was Britain's responsibility to provide and deliver all the equipment necessary and all the work was done in the United Kingdom. The final layout of the harbours—British and American—showed four main elements: the block ships, the floating breakwaters, and the

124

piers and pierheads. Many seemingly insuperable obstacles had to be overcome, apart from the shortage of labour, the need for tremendous quantities of concrete, of steel, and a thousand and one other items; but overcome they were. One of the greatest troubles was caused by the need to provide a pier which would ride safely up and down with the rise and fall of the tide of over 20 feet from a flat beach. The construction had to be strong enough to ride a gale and means to anchor it securely were essential. In 1943 a prototype pier and pierhead was built, which when put to the most severe sea tests stood up well. Production could now proceed with a degree of confidence.

SOME idea of the immense demands on building and engineering labour can be gauged by the fact that 20,000 workers were mobilised for the construction of the concrete caissons alone, and many more thousands were engaged on other parts, while large numbers of men and women in the steel and other industries strove to supply the enormous requirements of materials: it is estimated that 600,000 tons of cement and 75,000 tons of steel were used up. This was not all. Sites for construction work had to be found adjacent to waterways, and in the later stages men had to work at considerable heights and over water. All these efforts were spread throughout the country, as convenience served.

The need for speed demanded long and strenuous working hours in circumstances of every form of discomfort. In some instances the men had to carry on during air raids and by artificial light throughout the hours of darkness. But they never let up nor flinched. No hint of the nature of their work escaped to the public, and their great job was completed, as was that of the people making the many items of fitting necessary, on time. The rewards for these splendid services of the workers of Britain came to them in the success on D-day and the subsequent days.

Some weeks before D-day the pre-fabricated components of the harbours could be assembled and towed across the Channel, thanks to the vigilance of the Royal Air Force, immune from air attack. Yet there were many other things to consider and prepare. Experts of the Naval Meteorological Service predicted to the nearest foot the mean height of the breakers along the coast of Normandy, and how height would fluctuate with changes in the force and direction of the wind, and many other calculations had to be made with regard to sea and weather, conditions above and below the surface of the water, and so on.

Transportation of the huge blockships, the gigantic concrete caissons, and the floating breakwaters as well as the intricate pier equipment, was a task calling for more than ordinary skill. The various units had first to be towed from the places where they had been constructed to places of assembly on the south coast, sometimes long distances, as from Leith and Glasgow. And from these assembly points preparations were feverishly made for the risky and dangerous voyage across the hundred miles of the English Channel to the Normandy coast. How this was done has already become a legend. First to arrive were the blockships, which were successfully sunk in the required spots. The other parts followed, involving 210 tows of floating breakwaters, piers, and the huge caissons, in all a weight of nearly one million tons.

Port parties of Royal Engineers, or Seabees, landed on D-day, cleared mines, cut ramps in the esplanades and prepared roadways down to the beaches ready to receive the shore ends of the piers. The port party also included a naval beach commando and detachment from the Royal Marines. In the setting down of the harbour the soldiers and sailors worked hand in hand; soldiers were sailors and sailors were soldiers, and the Royal Marines were both. Their especial operations were finished by D-plus-12 day, by which time one pier hundreds of yards long with several pierheads was complete and coasters could be unloaded at any state of the tide.

To increase the difficulties a gale sprang up on the thirteenth day. Blowing hard from the north-east it struck the exposed harbours with great violence, smashing and disorganising much of the work in course of erection, and of the craft employed. Nevertheless, while unloading on the beaches elsewhere was impossible during this critical time, stores could still be landed from the artificial harbour, and troops also were able to go ashore. When the storm subsided it was found that the work of our engineers and workers had stood up well, a credit to all who had had a hand in

The colossal task of planning and constructing a pre-fabricated harbour involved the efforts of thousands of workers in many parts of the country. Here, in a busy shipyard, far from their final destination, concrete caissons to be used as breakwaters, are under construction. The caissons were fitted with seacocks so that they could be sunk in the sea at the point where they were to operate.

[*Crown Copyright Reserved*

This remarkable picture shows the linking up of "Mulberry" with the land on the other side. Powerful bull-dozers are making shore connections with the breakwater arm, and soon a complete and compact harbour will be formed. The size of each harbour is roughly the same as that of Dover. The planning of this enormous enterprise was so thorough that it took very little time to assemble off the French coast.

Here is a view of the join-up of the prefabricated port in use. This miracle harbour, with all its parts assembled, was completed by D-Day plus thirteen, and made possible the landing of men and supplies on such a scale as to ensure victory.

Shortly before its completion, an unprecedented storm arose which caused much damage to the floating dock. However, within a few days repairs were effected, and tanks and equipment were soon rolling inland.

the designing, construction and erection. Consequently, in spite of the worst gale in forty years, the Allied armies, and the enormous amount of stores that they required, were disembarked satisfactorily; and so was made possible the initial step to the liberation of Europe from the Nazi plague.

One of the most important features of "Mulberry" was the giant caissons. These caissons were made in six different sizes to suit various depths of water up to five and a half fathoms. The largest size had a displacement of 6044 tons, the smallest a displacement of 1672 tons. When floating, the whole looked rather like a Noah's Ark without its roof; there was no deck and so the cross walls gave the caisson the appearance of a huge egg-box when viewed from above. For use during the voyage, each caisson contained quarters for the crew of naval men who handled the ship, and the Royal Engineers (or Seabees) who were to carry out the operations of sinking the constructions in place.

At a later stage, Bofors guns, twenty tons of ammunition, and rough shelters for the gun-crews were placed on top of most of the caissons as additional anti-aircraft protection of the harbour. One large tug of about 1500 h.p. towed the empty caisson across the Channel. On arrival each was manœuvred into position with the help of smaller tugs. Then special valves were opened so that inflowing water filled the ship which settled down and sank as desired. It took roughly twenty-two minutes to sink the largest caissons. Of the various sizes there were sixty of the largest, and altogether 146 caissons, in the construction of which it was estimated that the following main materials were used: 330,000 cubic yards of concrete weighing nearly 660,000 tons; 31,000 tons of steel; and 1,500,000 super yards of shuttering.

The piers consisted of a single steel roadway carried on steel girders similar in many respects to those of an ordinary modern bridge. The design allowed of wide flexibility so that the heaving and twisting effect of the sea could be withstood. Each of the bridge spans was supported on special floats, some of steel and others of concrete, also designed to withstand the sea forces and also to sit down safely on rock or sand when the tide receded. Sections of pier were joined together by special

Another angle of "Mulberry" viewed along the pierheads and showing roadways leading off to the shore. It is wonderful to think how such a complicated task could be undertaken with such speed and secrecy.

A convoy of ambulances traversing the roadway to the pierhead. There was no delay in taking off wounded and transferring them to hospital ships to receive instant treatment.

means to give flexibility and to ensure connecting-up with ease and rapidity.

There was no limit to the length of a pier other than the depth of water for successful anchoring, but for towing, lengths of 480 feet were joined up. At the shore end these piers were joined to a very stout steel shallow draught float which could be pulled right inshore at high water. At the outer end they were linked to specially designed spud pierheads. These consisted of steel pontoons with a displacement of approximately 1000 tons. Each pierhead was a "ship" complete with crew's quarters, generating sets, storage accommodation and all essential equipment. Coasters berthed alongside and discharged their cargoes direct into lorries on the pierhead. Using the same pierhead, with some extra fittings, it could be converted for use by landing craft. A sort of false beach piece made of steel was provided on which the landing craft ran its bows and lowered its ramp. Vehicles could then run straight off and ashore very quickly by this means and without

more ado. These pierheads were constructed in various Scottish ports by some 240 contractors, involving the use of some 50,000 tons of steel.

The floating breakwater, which was of unusual worth during the stormy weather, consisted of floats incorporating 15,000 tons of steel. These floats were moored end to end in a long line. The units were pre-fabricated and then assembled at Southampton. Their object was to procure an area of comparatively calm water inside the harbour, so that the work of unloading might proceed at all times, uninterrupted.

By the skill and determination of the British experts, of the craftsmen, and the sea men, was made possible the success with which the Allied armies and their vital supplies were brought to France and landed on its beaches. It would not be too much to say that "Mulberry" was very largely responsible for the liberation of Europe and the victorious ending to the war. This feat will go down to history as one of the greatest military achievements of all times.

A busy scene at the artificial port. Motor transport is disembarking from a landing-stage to the pierhead, with the battlefield only a few miles away, and thus the Germans' main defence strategy—to hold the supply ports at any cost—was defeated.

Here is one of the piers which found its way in parts across the Channel to be assembled on the enemy's doorstep. Over it rattled tanks and guns, and all the equipment of war, which, but for this amazing achievement, would have been delayed at a time when every moment was vital.

# CURBING THE BARONS

THE idea of having a Parliament is very old. The name too, is very ancient. It means an assembly of people who have come to talk together. Long before Magna Carta, the great nobles used to assemble from time to time to discuss matters of national importance. Later they found it helpful to bring in the lesser nobles or "knights of the shire." There was, in each county, a " county court " to which all the freemen came to deal with affairs of common interest. Each county court was asked to send two knights to represent the county in Parliament.

These early Parliaments did not usually make laws; for in feudal times laws were generally established by custom, or were the result of decisions by the King's judges. The main purpose of Parliament in those days was to exchange ideas and information about what was going on in different parts of the country.

Probably the oldest municipal hall in the country, the ancient Guild Hall at Exeter, county town of Devon. Dating back to Elizabethan times, it has a wonderful roof with gilded beams. It was once the centre for the powerful incorporated companies or guilds.

## SIMON de MONTFORT

Soon after Magna Carta, an important change took place. Just as the barons had wished to limit the King's power, so the smaller lords and the towns wanted to set a limit to the power of the barons. Some fifty years after Magna Carta these smaller lords rose in rebellion. Their leader was Simon de Montfort, Earl of Leicester. In 1265, during a short period when he was victorious, he called a Parliament which included very few of the great lords. Most of its members were either knights of the shire, or (now sent for the first time) members elected by the chartered towns. De Montfort was defeated and killed in battle in the next year, but the idea of his Parliament remained.

In 1297, Edward I, in desperate need of money, gave to a Parliament, elected in this way, a promise that no new taxes would be imposed without the approval of Parliament. In previous Parliaments the members from the shires and towns, sitting among the assembled great lords, had taken little part in the proceedings. Now they felt that, if they were to be asked to approve new taxes, they should give their approval only if their grievances were heard and remedied. It soon became the rule that before any taxes were approved, the complaints of the shires and towns must be heard and remedies promised. The great lords having no interest in these grievances, made it their practice to sit in a separate chamber. So it came about that there are two Houses of Parliament, the Lords and the Commons.

Even so, Parliament was weak when faced

with a strong King. It remained so for several hundred years. Kingship was much feared and respected and the value of Parliament was little appreciated. Towns and shires often complained of the expense of sending members to Westminster and petitioned the King to be excused. Sometimes they had to be compelled to send their members.

## RULE BY CONSENT

When the Wars of the Roses—that seemingly endless civil strife between the rival families of York and Lancaster—came to an end with the victory of Henry VII at Bosworth. Henry, having obtained the throne by force of arms and not by right of birth, felt the need of some legal authority for his kingship. The Pope refused to confer " divine authority " and so Henry went to Parliament and asked for a vote of approval so as to show that he ruled " with the consent of the law and the people of England." His son Henry VIII did the same, and found it convenient to use Parliament for other purposes. His various marriages and divorces led to quarrels with the Church and made difficulties over the succession to the throne. He asked Parliament to name him as Head of the Church, and to approve his choice as to which of his children should succeed him as king. All this gave to Parliament a much more important place in national affairs.

## KING v PARLIAMENT

The Parliaments of Queen Elizabeth at times became restive. England was going

King Charles I, the romantic if incautious monarch who ended his life on the scaffold.

The Earl of Strafford, one of King Charles I's closest advisers, on his way to execution. Painted by Paul de la Roche in 1797.

through a difficult time; feudal ways were disappearing, there was much poverty, and there were fierce differences over religion. All this discontent Elizabeth, by her own personality, managed to keep in check, but her successor, James of Scotland, had no experience of Parliamentary methods. He believed he was King by divine right and could do just as he pleased. Parliament, of course, resisted him, and throughout his reign and that of his son Charles I, a bitter quarrel grew. In 1628 Parliament presented to Charles I a Petition of Right which made various claims somewhat like those of Magna Carta. The Petition said that money ought to be raised only by taxes approved by Parliament, and that neither the King, nor his Privy Council (who were appointed by him, not elected by the people), had the right to make laws. Nor had the Star Chamber (a committee of the

Oliver Cromwell, the fanatical puritan who became Lord Protector of the Realm.

over twenty-one years old. A group called the " Levellers " put forward demands for greater equality between rich and poor. When Cromwell died, after ruling as " Protector " (a kind of Dictator) for several years, the moderate parliamentary leaders were afraid of these extremists. They joined with their old Royalist enemies and brought in Charles II as King, hoping that he would preserve law and order and the rights of property. Charles had to agree that all his Ministers of State and advisers should be approved by Parliament and that Parliament should remain in control of taxation and the army.

Charles II managed to play off against each other, the various groups (merchants, bankers and landowners) in Parliament and in the country, and so kept a good deal of personal power. His brother, James II, tried to carry personal rule too far. He took away the charters of the towns and issued new ones which allowed him (and not the towns-people) to choose their Members of Parliament. He was driven into exile.

Parliament then invited his daughter Mary and her husband, William of Orange, a Dutch prince, to be Queen and King. Parliament, in a Bill of Rights, laid down that the

Privy Council) any right to bring citizens to trial and punishment, instead of through the ordinary courts of justice. The King granted the Petition, and Parliament in return granted the King some of the money he demanded. This was not the end of the quarrel.

Charles tried for many years to rule on his own but at last the need for money compelled him to summon Parliament. One of its first actions was to "impeach" the King's chief Minister of State, Lord Strafford, that is, declare him a traitor and condemn him to death. The King then tried to dissolve Parliament by force, and arrested some of its leaders. Civil war broke out in which eventually the parliamentary armies, under Oliver Cromwell, won. Charles I was beheaded.

## CONTROL OF TAXATION

The winning side then, itself, became disunited. The army wanted great reforms, including a Parliament elected every two years by all citizens

This old print shows where the Star Chamber met in the Royal Palace of Westminster.

powers of the King, in relation to taxation, judges, courts of law, and the army, were to be used only with the consent of Parliament. Later they even decided who was to be the next King.

This situation has remained more or less the same since that time. Parliament makes the laws, authorises taxes, and decides what the taxes shall be spent upon. The carrying out of the laws and management of the army and other national services are looked after by Ministers appointed by the King. This body of Ministers, called the Cabinet, is the real government of the country, but it can only function with the consent of Parliament. Without the support of Parliament the Government cannot get money and cannot make laws. For this reason, it has become the rule that the King shall choose his Ministers from among those Members of Parliament who are likely to be supported by a majority of the votes of their fellow members. This relationship between King and Parliament is what people have in mind when they say that our country has a "Constitutional Monarchy."

Parliament has, therefore, since the time of William and Mary, been the controlling force in national government. Those who can manage to control Parliament become the real rulers of the country.

## PEOPLE POORLY REPRESENTED

For very many years after William and Mary, Parliament did not properly represent the people of England. A few members were elected by the people of the towns and by the freemen of the counties, but in most cases members got elected by bribing the voters. Towns like this were called "rotten boroughs" or "pocket boroughs," because all the voters were usually bribed by some rich man to vote the way he wanted—he had

the borough "in his pocket." When George III came to the throne in 1760 he made a great effort to obtain personal power. He saw that to do this he would need control of the House of Commons. He spent a great deal of money in bribing members of Parliament to vote the way he told them. They even voted him money which he spent on further bribery. This went on for twenty years or so until, as a result of the American War of Independence which was largely brought on by the incompetence of George and his Ministers, England lost her American colonies. There was a great cry for reform both from Parliament itself and from the people.

## PARLIAMENTARY REFORMERS

The demands of the reformers were that many more people should have the right to vote, that pocket boroughs and rotten boroughs should be done away with, and that no Member of Parliament should be in the pay of the King.

At one time in England even religious houses were fortified. Palace Eye Gateway, entrance to the Bishop's Palace, Wells, Somerset.

The movement towards reform was, however, checked by the French Revolution, which started in 1789. Responsible people in England feared that if the ordinary people were given more power England would turn revolutionary like the France of that time, with all its terror and bloodshed. During the Napoleonic Wars which followed the French Revolution, Parliament became rather tyrannous and oppressive in its efforts to prevent revolutionary ideas from spreading in England. Some of the rights and freedom gained in the past were for a time lost again. But reform was only postponed. The year 1832, with the passing of the first Reform Bill, saw the beginning of great changes both in national and in local government.

The developments from then until now will be left to another chapter.

These young pygmies, outside their primitive huts, are fascinated by the camera, and, like youngsters all the world over, are eager to watch anything new and strange.

# WHERE THE PYGMIES LIVE

THE pygmies! How the old writers of adventure stories loved them! Savage dwarfs with poisoned arrows closing in silently on the explorers' camp somewhere in the jungles of central Africa. Let us see what they are really like; where and how they live to-day.

Look at a map of Africa; quite a small one will do. Find the Equator, which cuts across the continent about half-way down. Starting from the right, or eastern end, run your finger along it. Your finger will travel across Kenya; it will enter Uganda, and cross the northern tip of Lake Victoria, which is half as big as the whole of England. Then it will enter the Congo, and soon you will see Stanleyville, an important town which is actually just above the Equator line. Between Stanleyville and the Uganda border lies the great Ituri Forest, and this is the central stronghold of the pygmies. Your finger will have travelled about one thousand two hundred miles from where it started on the coast.

## TREES TWO HUNDRED FEET HIGH

From Uganda, a road runs through the forest to Stanleyville. It is narrow, and rough, and tall grass grows between the wheel-tracks. For four hundred miles you travel at the bottom of a gorge, for the forest rises in high green walls on either side. The trees are sometimes two hundred feet high; they are tangled and festooned with creepers, and they meet overhead, so that it is gloomy and sunless. But it is very hot. Voices echo thinly here, as they do in some great cathedral, and the tree-trunks tower upwards like pillars.

You will see your first pygmies at the road-sides. Wherever you stop in Africa, no matter how wild and deserted the country seems to be, a little group of natives always appears. The pygmies don't look a bit like dwarfs; nor are they savage. They are about the size of a well-built boy of twelve to fourteen. In fact, they are perfectly proportioned, miniature men.

At first, if you stop the car, they approach cautiously; you can see they are ready to run

Every ten miles or so there is a village at the roadside. These belong to normal-sized Africans, and each one has a community of pygmies attached to it. The pygmies are skilful hunters, but they have no idea of growing things, so they keep the village supplied with

Full-grown pygmies beside a white woman of average size. The "little people," in perfect proportion, are about the size of a well-built boy of fourteen.

away. But if you grin at them and wave your hand, they come up smiling and chattering, and examine you and all your possessions. They are certainly not embarrassed. If they think you are wearing a funny hat, one will point at it, and they will all go off into peals of good-natured laughter. On one occasion I pointed the oil-can at them accidently, and they all fled with cries of alarm!

But they loved having their photographs taken; and they were delighted when I gave them the camera, being careful not to show them the lever. They took turns at "photographing" each other; they must have taken a hundred in five minutes. They were very disappointed when I couldn't produce them immediately from the camera.

meat in return for various fruits and vegetables. They are really almost the servants of the other Africans. However, they are well treated, because if they were not they would move to another village immediately.

## A VILLAGE BUILT IN FOUR HOURS

The huts by the roadside are big and square, and thatched with huge leaves. They are, of course, hemmed in by thick jungle. There is always a long, low shelter in the middle of the clearing; a log fire burns there, round which the men lie in the evening. The pygmies are not allowed under this. Their huts are tiny things shaped like bee-hives. They simply stick a circle of twigs into the ground, bend the tops towards the centre, and fasten them.

Though shy, these sturdy pygmy children were eventually persuaded to have their photograph taken.

except the bark of a certain tree. They take a small piece and beat it out with wooden mallets. After many hours of patient hammering the bark becomes like a sheet of thin, brown linen, many times its original size. They often decorate it with red and blue dyes made from forest plants.

## A DIET OF BANANAS

Besides the meat they obtain from hunting, their principal food is bananas. They eat the sweet yellow one that we know, and also another large green one called a plantain, which is used for cooking only. It is starchy rather than sweet, and you would have difficulty in deciding whether you were eating a fruit or a vegetable.

The pygmies have never learnt the art of making fire, though they often see the other tribes doing it. They rely on their " everlasting fire "—a small log which will smoulder for days without going out or breaking into flame.

They thatch this framework with leaves. A whole village is built in about four hours.

Although it is shady beneath the great trees, it is generally very hot. Every morning the sun melts the thick night mist which lies over the tree-tops, and the forest drips and glistens. Do you know that thick, wet heat in a small bathroom just after someone has had a very hot bath? It is just like that in the green depths of the Ituri Forest. There is no summer and winter. The trees are dropping leaves and growing new ones all the year round. At certain times of the year there is a definite wet season. Then sheet lightning darts and flickers in a purple-black sky; thunder peals in echoing crashes; and the trees rock and creak in sudden wind-storms. The pygmies curl up in their little shelters, as rain beats on the frail roofs.

They wear, men and women, just a little skirt of bark-cloth. They have no wool, no cotton, nothing of which to make clothes

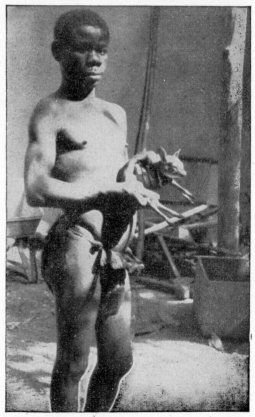

The pygmy is holding a young duiker which he has caught in the Ituri Forest.

There are always plenty of these logs in the village, and if they go out hunting they wrap a piece in large leaves, and carry it with them. Then they only have to pile twigs on it and blow, and they have a hot fire in a very few minutes.

Funnily enough, they do not think we are at all clever to have things like watches and rifles and cameras. They certainly think these things are wonderful, but they say, " You have better ' medicine ' than we have. Our gods have given us bows and arrows and bark-cloth; yours have given you all these marvellous things." They just think we are lucky; they don't admire our ingenuity in making these things at all!

One pygmy I knew had been given a pair of sun-spectacles with pink rims. He was very proud of these and always wore them, although in the dim light under the trees he must have had the greatest difficulty in seeing where he was going! A cigarette is a great treat. They all smoke if they get the chance, from the old women to the small children. They smoke in quick little puffs like a railway engine starting from a station, and the cigarette is soon gone. Indeed, another tribe of very small men, the bushmen of the Kalahari desert in South Africa, have such good lungs a cigarette vanishes in two puffs. One long puff—half the cigarette gone; two—and only the stub-end is left!

Yes, the pygmies are simple, very happy people, though they have a hard struggle to win the necessities of life from the great forest around them.

# HOW THE PYGMIES LIVE

THE pygmies of the Ituri Forest spend nearly all their time hunting. They do not look upon it as a sport; it is a matter of grim, day-to-day necessity. If the hunters come back empty-handed after many hours in the forest, there is nothing for them or the waiting women and children to eat.

The forest, in spite of the wild profusion of its growth, provides little or nothing that is eatable. You cannot go out and pick fruit or dig up wild vegetables. Before any crop can be grown, giant trees have to be felled and masses of tough creeper hacked down. The pygmies have always preferred hunting to this immense labour.

There is no grass, so domestic animals such as cattle or goats cannot be kept. The lack of grass also means that only those animals which can live on leaves are found in such country. The great herds of game roam the open plains of Africa; they could not exist in the forest.

## AN ANTELOPE AS SMALL AS A CAT

What is there then? The most important animals to the pygmies are small antelopes called duikers. There are a number of varieties, the smallest being only about the size of a cat when fully-grown. There are elephants; and that strange and rare animal called the okapi.

It is related to the giraffe, and looks like a tall deer with a pointed face. It is found in the Ituri Forest, and nowhere else in the world. This is also true of the giant gorilla, though smaller monkeys are common throughout the forest.

The pygmies are experts with the bow and arrow. The bows are very small—they look almost like toy ones—for a large bow would be unusable among the trees. The bow-string is made from tough creeper, and the flights of the little arrows are strips of leaf, not feathers. The arrows are steel-tipped, though in the case of a difficult shot they use a poisoned arrow, which has a sharp wood tip. The poison is made from a small plant. The pygmies wrap the tip carefully in leaves, in case anyone should be accidentally scratched.

For food, they rely mainly on net-hunting. I once went out on a net-hunt with them. We started in the early morning; about twenty men straggled out of the village behind the headman, each one carrying a rolled net twenty yards long. These nets are made from the fibres of plants, for the pygmies have no twine or cord of any sort. They moved silently, in small, rapid strides along a narrow trail. I soon realised why pygmies are so small! Being a foot and a half taller than they were, I was bent double most of the time, bumping my

This animal, which looks as if it had strayed from a pantomime, is the okapi, which is to be found only in the Ituri Forest in Central Africa. It is related to the giraffe.

head on branches and scratching my face on twigs.

## LAYING THE TRAIL

As we went along in the steamy heat, the head-man bent over twigs to show those who were following which way we had gone. Sometimes he placed a large leaf across the entrance to a side trail, which meant they were not to go that way. He did not speak or shout. If he wished to summon anybody, he crooked one arm and hit the outside of his bent elbow with the cupped palm of his other hand. This made a sharp " plop " which carried distinctly through the undergrowth, but did not alarm the animals as a shout would have done.

We went on and on through a maze of greenery, till I had utterly lost my sense of direction. The women had gone out separately; their job was to beat through the forest, driving the animals on to the nets. It was all a marvel of organisation, and completely puzzling to me, because when the men started to pay out the nets through the trees they all knew the precise direction they had to face. And the women, a mile away, knew exactly where the nets were. I peered about in the undergrowth, wondering at this sixth sense, while the men adjusted the nets.

They hung them from low branches, or cut nicks in tree-trunks to which they hitched the top strand. End to end, the nets stretched through the forest for some four hundred yards. The timing of it was wonderful, too, for no sooner were the nets ready than I heard the shrill, distant voices of the women, as they started to advance through the undergrowth in a long line. The poor women always get the hardest jobs in Africa!

The men crouched behind the nets, tense and silent. The cries of the women grew louder. Then there were rustlings and one or two quick scuffles. As the animals dashed through the trees into the nets the men pounced upon them. They were dispatched swiftly and mercifully. The nets were quickly rolled up; men and women filed down different trails farther into the forest, to make the next cast. They

The pygmies are expert with bow and arrows. These weapons are small for easy handling in the dense undergrowth. The arrows are mainly steel-tipped, though on occasions they use poisoned arrows with a sharp wood tip. The poison is made from a small plant.

would probably make six to eight in all before the day was out. As for me, I was already soaked, bedraggled and weary. I returned to the village, guided by an old man.

## THE CROCODILE'S WEAK SPOT

Many rivers wind through the forest on their way to join the mighty Congo. If the pygmies are hard-pressed for food they go fishing. Their favourite way, because it is the easiest, is to throw small bundles of poisonous twigs into a still pool. These stupefy the fish, which float to the surface where the fishermen are waiting for them. And there may be something waiting for the fishermen too—a crocodile! One man, with great scars on his leg, told me how it had been seized by one of these evil monsters. It started to pull him into deep water, but he snatched at an overhanging branch desperately, and hung on to it. Just as he felt his strength was giving out, he remembered something his old grandfather had told him. " Then I let go with one hand," the man with the scars said, " and dug my thumb as hard as I could into the crocodile's eye." It let go immediately and vanished.

The pygmy spends most of his life hunting. When he is not doing this, or preparing his weapons, it is safe to say he will be either sleeping, talking, singing, or dancing. As the

Despite his size, the elephant is not always safe from pygmy hunters.

sun sinks and the warm tropical night descends on the village, you will see the women cooking at small fires outside the huts; the girls " making up " each others' faces, drawing patterns of blue lines on cheeks and forehead; the men sharpening their knives or re-stringing their bows.

Suddenly the muffled beat of a skin drum starts. The sound is nothing like the sharp tattoo of the drums of a military band. It is a quite soft, throbbing sound which carries for long distances through the forest. Indeed, villages talk to one another by beating their drums, sending messages by altering the rhythms.

## HOW THE PYGMIES DANCE

Everyone dances. Many of the men put on small hats with feathers in them, rather like absurd little coronets. They go on for hours, jigging and jumping round the clearing in a long line. It gets rather boring for the onlooker eventually, for there is little variation. But the pygmies leap about happily and excitedly till they gleam with sweat from head to foot in the firelight. Sometimes one will break out of the line and do a violent solo dance with loud cries and yells. Anyone can make up his own steps; the pygmies' dances are not the highly organised affairs of many African tribes. It is just a jolly and free-and-easy way of " letting off steam."

To our ears, a pygmy choir makes a very strange noise. One man sings a solo in a piping, cracked voice, while the rest sing a queer, half-whispered accompaniment. It reminded me of something I could not quite place. One evening I suddenly realised what it was. As soon as night falls, all the myriads of insects and frogs in the forest set up a shrill chorus; the air is full of clinkings and whirrings and tinny pipings. There is always a frog or cricket close to you whose voice stands out above all the rest. I am sure the pygmies' song was in imitation of this. After all, it is the only music they know.

Whether they are singing or dancing, they go on far into the night, till the fires have died down. Then they crawl into their leaf huts. The insect chorus of the Ituri Forest takes over till dawn, while the slow, winking lights of fireflies float across the clearing above the sleeping pygmies.

# THE PATIENT PLODDING PLOUGHMAN

[Robert McLeod

This fine camera study shows the photographer's art at its best. It has been taken at an angle to display an attractive background of sky, with the " human interest," the man and his horses, forming the centre of the picture in the foreground. Note the wonderful cloud formations.

[Will F. Taylor

A group of African schoolboys at drill in their playground, learning how to salute smartly. The story of the salute, and how it came into being, is explained below.

# DO YOU KNOW?

## by LAVINIA DERWENT

*Do you know that a fish can climb a tree?*

Most fishes, as we know, cannot live without water. Indeed we often speak of people who are out of their natural element being like "fish out of water." If a fish is brought out of its natural element it gasps for a time and then dies, because as soon as its gills cease to be wet it cannot breathe.

But there is one strange fish which often leaves the water, travels inland and actually climbs trees. It is called the Climbing Perch and lives in Burma, Ceylon and India.

This fish always has a good reason for leaving its watery home. It never thinks of roaming unless it fears there is a drought at hand, and that the pool or river where it is lying may dry up.

The climbing perch does not want to be stranded, so it sets out to look for a deeper pool or river. It has spiney fins which help it to "walk" over the land in search of a new home.

Why does the perch not die as any other fish would if it were out of water? The answer is

that at each side of its head it has a kind of store-cupboard where it can hoard up supplies of water. This keeps its gills moist, and gives it a chance to breathe until it has reached the safety of another pool.

Perhaps the perch may be a long time in finding a new pool. If this happens the wise little fish knows that there is often water to be found in the hollow of a tree. It keeps this as a last hope, and if its store of water is nearly at an end, it begins to climb up the tree.

It clings to the bark with its gill-covers, and uses its spiney fins to help it to climb. The journey is very slow, but at last the perch reaches its goal, and is rewarded by finding the precious water which means new life to it.

*Why do soldiers salute?*

Do you ever wonder why soldiers salute by raising their hands smartly to their heads?

This is a very old custom. The origin of it is said to date back to the Middle Ages. In those days the knights often took part in contests to try their skill in using the spear and the lance. At these contests a lady was chosen to be Queen, and to give the prizes to the knights.

When they went up to her throne they shielded their eyes with their hands, as though her beauty dazzled them. This became a token of respect, and has now come into general use.

## Do you know that there is a skeleton in your bathroom?

It seems queer to say that you have skeletons in your bathroom or kitchen, but it is true. A skeleton is the bones or frame of an animal, bird, fish or other creature that lives. How can you use such a thing in the home? You use it when washing and taking your bath. The skeletons are the sponge and the loofah.

The sponge once rested on the bed of the ocean. It was then a living animal, that ate and drank and grew. If you look at a sponge you will see that it is full of holes, some large and others very small. When alive the sponge takes in sea-water and very tiny sea-creatures through its pores. These are the smallest holes. Then the waste water is sent out through the large holes.

People dive down into the sea to pick the

[Shepstone
This seasoned old lady, while enjoying her pipe, is clipping and cleaning sponges lately brought up from the sea bed by divers, in the Bahamas.

sponges. These divers are very fine swimmers and can stay under the water a long time. The sponges are then washed, and the skeletons of the sea-animals are sent to the shops to become very useful helps in the bathroom.

The other skeleton, harder and stronger than the sponge, is the loofah. This is really a vegetable sponge, for it once grew on a tree called the Egyptian Luffa. It is really a gourd, a long fruit like a cucumber or a vegetable marrow.

The fruit of the luffa tree is gathered, and the pulp and seeds are squeezed out. The skeleton that remains is then dried, and it becomes the loofah we know.

The loofah is used for scrubbing the body when washing or bathing, and it helps to freshen the skin. The sponge is used when gentle washing is needed. That is why mother uses a sponge when washing baby.

## How many hairs are in your head?

It would be difficult to tell exactly how many hairs are in your head; but it has been estimated that a brown-haired man has 109,000 hairs, and a fair-haired man 140,000 hairs.

Dark brown hair is the most common in Britain. Each hair varies from the 250th to the 600th part of an inch in thickness.

It has been proved that a single hair will support a weight of about four ounces. Hundreds of years ago the Chinese and Japanese used to make rope from hair. One of these hair-ropes is in the British Museum. It is several thousand feet long and weighs about two tons.

## Why does a bee sting?

When a bee stings you, the hurt you receive is nothing to the injury caused to the insect, for, once its sting has been delivered, the bee dies. The sting is really a sharp barbed tube through which the bee sends a drop of poisonous matter. The barb is torn away from the bee's body, injuring it so badly that it dies in a very short time. You will realise, therefore, that bees are not particularly anxious to use their weapon of defence, and it is only when they are in a very tight corner that they will produce their sting.

In this story there is a rather wonderful moral, showing us that the bee has to restrain its anger on the penalty of death, and that it is only because of our offensive attacks on it that it loses its life.

*Photos :*] [*Mondiale*

This hungry little squirrel has dug up some of his hidden store and, in a sunny period during the winter, has wakened from his winter sleep to satisfy his hunger. Below is seen a desert scene, showing the distant skyline over the waste of sand.

## How does a fly walk upside down?

Have you ever watched a fly walking on the ceiling and wondered how it could keep its balance? The answer is that the fly has a little pad on the end of each foot, which is hollow in the middle. This makes a suction when the foot is pressed on a surface, and keeps the fly from falling.

Flies have another useful gift. Their eyes consist of thousands of very small eyes, and the flies can therefore see in all directions.

## How many bones are in your body?

There are 206 bones in your body, each one playing an important part.

You have 12 pairs of ribs, and 33 bones in your spine. There are 8 bones in the skull and 14 in the face. The only movable one of all these is the lower jawbone.

The outside of a bone is very hard, but the inside is full of cells. Some long straight bones are hollow and contain marrow. This is a fatty substance.

There are 527 muscles in your body. In your jaw alone there are 8 muscles. These are very powerful, and when fully developed can exert a force of about 500 pounds. No machine is as wonderfully designed as is your body.

## Where do colours come from?

We know that there are seven colours in the rainbow. These are violet, indigo, blue, green, yellow, orange and red. But do you know where we find the colouring matter from which we get paints, and with which we dye our clothes?

Some of these colours come from insects, others from plants, and some from stones and coal.

A tiny insect called the cochineal, which lives in Mexico, gives us scarlet, carmine and crimson. Green can be obtained from berries of the buckthorn. Sepia is obtained in a strange manner from the cuttle-fish. It is put out by the fish to act as a smoke-screen when it is attacked.

Many dyes are made from vegetables and plants. In bygone days the ancient Britons used to paint their bodies with woad. This was a kind of blue dye which they extracted from a plant. It is sometimes used to-day to improve the colour of other blue dyes.

Gamboge is the sap of a tree which grows in Siam. Prussian blue is made from horses' hooves, and many other colours come from coal-tar, which is one of the most amazing of all substances.

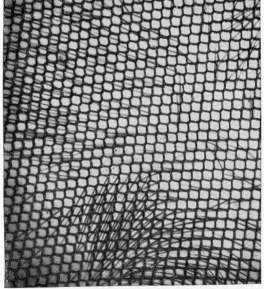 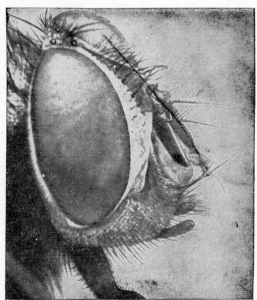

*Photos:]* [*Mondiale*

The highly magnified section of a fly's eye (left) shows some of the 4000 facets which enable the insect to see in all directions. An enlarged picture of the fly's head and eye is shown on the right. The fly has many enemies in the insect world, while the spiders and most human beings are always on its track. The fly spreads disease, and therefore he is everybody's enemy. No wonder he needs such efficient eyes!

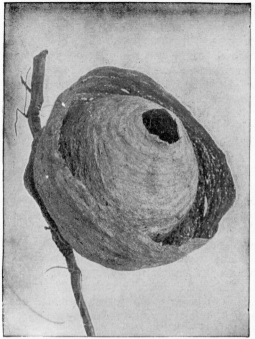 

Photos :] [Mondian

The wasp makes wood fibre into a pulp, just as man makes paper. Inside the nest combs are made, much as those made by the bee. Here the wasps are seen busy at work on their combs.

In the Scottish Highlands, the weavers make their own dyes from plants and vegetables. They have their own recipes, which are handed down from one branch of the family to the other.

The Chinese, too, make a dye known as Indian ink. This is manufactured from lamp-black and glue.

*Who taught man to make paper?*

Man learned to make paper through watching a clever insect at work. This busy insect was the wasp, who makes a rough kind of paper with which it builds its nest.

This little paper-maker uses wood fibres which he takes from trees with his strong jaws and then pulps up with his saliva. This forms a kind of paste with which he builds his cell and the outer cover of his nest.

To-day man has followed his example and now makes paper in much the same way.

*Are you ever nervous?*

All of us have bundles of nerves in our bodies. Without them we would not be able to see or hear, or feel or smell.

These nerves look like fine white threads or fibres. The brain and spinal cord are the central part of this nervous system. The matter they are made of is known as nervous matter. From these centres bundles of nerve-fibres spread all over the body.

Nerves are like tiny messengers which send instructions to the brain. If we want to move our hands or to run or eat, the nerves take the message to the brain, which sets the proper machinery in motion.

We know that the brain is the home of the mind, and from here comes all our thoughts and wishes. The nerves carry the news of everything we see or hear to the brain. Indeed, all we do, say, or think puts these busy nerves in motion.

*Why do we count in tens?*

We count up to ten and then to twenty, and so on, and talk of units—tens (ten units), hundreds (ten tens), thousands (ten hundreds).

How did this come about? If you look at your hands you will find the clue. How many fingers and thumbs have you altogether? Ten.

In olden days men counted on their fingers, as do many savage tribes of natives to-day. They thus counted to ten, and then made a mark, perhaps on the ground, to show "one ten." Then they began to count another ten.

It is said that one tribe could count hundreds by a clever way. Three men sat down together and a fourth man sat opposite them. The three men held up their hands with fingers outstretched. The fourth man counted the first man's fingers once—that made ten. Then he doubled down the first finger of the middle man. When he had counted another ten on the first man's fingers, he doubled the next finger of the middle man down.

When he had counted ten tens the middle man had all his fingers closed, and the first finger of the third man was doubled down to show "one ten-tens" or one hundred. Thus these natives could count up to one hundred.

Rather clever, is it not?

## How do we know that the earth is round?

We know that the earth is round because if we set off on a journey westwards round the world we at last return to our starting point.

The earth moves round the sun, turning on its axis as it does so. Thus we get day and night. Day is the time when our half of the world is facing the sun. As the part of the earth where we live comes round to meet the sun we see the sun peeping over the horizon. This is morning. Then as we turn more towards the sun the day goes on to midday, or noon. Now our part of the earth begins to pass away from the sun's rays, and we have evening and night.

If you watch a ship going out to sea you will at last see it "sink" over the horizon. This is because it is disappearing over the curved edge of the round earth's surface.

## Can we hear every sound?

There are sounds too low or too high for us to hear. Insects and animals can hear them, but their pitch does not penetrate the ears of human beings.

The squeal of a baby mouse, for example, might never reach our ears, though other mice can hear it at once. Bats, also, have a high-pitched note which is difficult for us to pick up.

Even very small insects have organs of hearing which differ from ours and which can pick up faint notes that would never reach our ears.

Animals have a very keen sense of hearing. All cats, from the tiger to the tomcat, can hear

sounds that we would never detect. This helps them when they are out hunting, to guess when danger is at hand, or to find out their prey.

## Why do we shake hands when we meet?

In olden days there were no lighted streets and no policemen. Thieves lurked about in the dark and men carried swords for defence. When two men met it was the custom for them to hold each other's weapon hands (that is, their right hands) to show that there was no weapon there and that they meant to be friendly.

When they were gripping each other's hands they knew there could be no danger from one another. Thus, through time, men came to regard the holding of each other's hands as a greeting and a sign of friendship.

The Chinaman shakes his own hand when he meets you. The Maoris of New Zealand rub noses when they meet. White men, however, still hold out the right hand when they greet one another.

## How do birds find their way?

We often marvel at the clever way in which the birds can find their way across the sea to the warm lands where they spend the winter. They have very keen eyesight and an instinct which seems to guide them safely on their travels. When they are flying over land, birds follow the rivers or coastline whenever they can. They seem to remember routes which they have followed before and are able to find their way without difficulty.

Birds fly at a great height when they are migrating. Some fly at a speed of from 40 to 100 miles an hour. The swift, which is so-called because of its swift flight, can exceed 100 miles an hour; and the hawk, which can fly at 150 miles an hour, is the swiftest of all.

The bird which makes the longest journey is the Arctic Tern. Every year it flies from the Arctic regions to the Antarctic and back again. The total distance of this amazing journey is 22,000 miles.

## Who is the man in the moon?

Often when we look at the moon we think that we can see the eyes, nose and mouth of a man. Some people think that he is leaning on a fork, on which he carries a bundle of sticks. Others imagine that they can see a dog by his

[*Shepstone*

When we look at the figures standing near the trees on the left and right of this picture, we begin to realise the tremendous size of the giant redwood trees of California. These are the oldest living things in our modern world.

side. What we are really seeing are the shadows caused by the deep craters on the moon's surface.

If we looked at the moon through a telescope we would see mountains and clefts. There are nearly forty of these mountains higher than Mont Blanc and many deep craters which help to form pictures of the "man in the moon."

The diameter of the moon is 2,160 miles. Forty-nine moons could therefore be placed in the earth.

### What is the oldest thing alive?

The oldest living things in the world, and the highest, are the giant Redwood trees. Some of these are still growing in California, where they first began life about five thousand years ago.

These monster trees are something like our own pines and firs, and bear cones just as they do. But our own species could never reach the amazing height and strength of these forest kings.

Some of them are over 340 feet high, which is at least three times the height of the biggest tree in this country. The leaves are small, and look like scales which overlap on the branches

and twigs. One of these trees has been known to produce ten thousand planks of fine timbe each ten feet in length.

In a grove of these giant Redwoods a tunnel has been made through the trunk of one of the trees, so that motorists can drive through the archway. It is amazing to think that one small seed can grow into such a monster.

### Is Friday a lucky day?

Friday, the sixth day of the week, is named after Frig or Friga, the wife of the god Odin. It is a day kept sacred as a fast day by both Eastern and Western Churches.

Friday is often thought to be an unlucky day, because Good Friday, the day before Easter, was the day set apart for the Crucifixion.

Legend also says that Friday was the day on which Adam was born, and received into Paradise. It was also the day on which he was expelled, and the day on which he died.

Many other Fridays have proved unlucky, and have been called Black Fridays. On one of these unlucky days a great bank in London failed. On another the news reached London that the Pretender had reached as far as Derby.

All kinds of fairies and elves, according to

legend, are changed to hideous animals on Friday, and are forced to remain like that until Monday.

In England there is a proverb that a Friday full moon brings foul weather. Another old saying is: "He who laughs on Friday will weep on Sunday."

Columbus, however, seems to have found Friday a lucky day. He set out on his voyage of discovery on a Friday, and he first sighted land on another Friday. It was on Friday the 13th of June that he discovered the continent of America.

### How far can a kangaroo leap?

The kangaroo is the star leaper in the animal world. He can jump 70 feet without effort, and has been known to clear a 15-foot fence.

The springbok, a member of the antelope family, is another clever jumper. He will leap 12 feet into the air, with the greatest of ease.

Lions, tigers and leopards are all fine jumpers. Even the Morocco goat can clear a fence 12 feet high.

Although horses are known to be good jumpers, their record falls far behind that of

Robinson Crusoe rows ashore from the wreck, to begin his marvellous adventures on the island.

the kangaroo. The longest jump by a horse is 37 feet.

### Why has a golf ball a patterned surface?

It has been found that when a ball is knocked or thrown through the air it will go farther if not smooth. The air bumps against the small depressions or sunken parts of the design and makes the ball spin as it flies. This helps it to go farther and keep better on its course.

Bullets and shells fired from rifles and guns are made to twist as they fly. The barrels of the guns and rifles have a screw thread or twist cut on their insides. The bullet or shell travels up the screw and is spun round, so that it whirls and bores its way through the air.

### Who was the real "Robinson Crusoe"?

Daniel Defoe wrote the famous story which tells of the adventures of Robinson Crusoe on a desert island.

One day in Bristol he met a Scottish seaman, called Alexander Selkirk. This man had been wrecked on a desert island and told Defoe of his adventures. The tale was so interesting that Defoe made up his mind to write it in a book and to add to it from his own imagination.

Thus the story of Robinson Crusoe came about, and has become so popular with young and old that it has been translated into nearly every living language.

### Why do we call them newspapers?

The word *news*, meaning information about the day's happenings, had a queer beginning.

When newspapers were first printed, the four points of the compass—N for North, S for South, E for East and W for West—were printed on the top of the sheet. This was to show that the stories told in the papers came from all parts of the world.

One day the owner of a newspaper began to play about with the letters NSEW, and changed them to spell NEWS. He printed this in big letters on the top of his paper. It made a word, and other papers copied the idea.

Thus the name newspaper came into being.

### What is an echo?

There is an old Greek legend which tells how a nymph named Echo was punished for some misdeed by not being able to speak for herself.

She could only repeat what anyone said to her.

In the same way we often hear our own words coming back to us, and when we do, we call them echoes.

An echo is caused by the waves of sound meeting some even surface such as a wall of a building. The sound is turned back on its course, causing an echo which reaches us a moment later. Sound travels so swiftly, at the rate of 1125 feet in a second, that the echo can be heard almost as soon as we have spoken.

Many woods, rocks and mountains produce natural echoes, and some places have become famous for their strange powers of "speaking back."

[*Mondiale*

Here two ants have met and are exchanging their news by vibrations, which are interpreted by their feelers, or antennae.

### Can insects and birds talk to each other?

Insects have their own ways of talking to each other. They do not depend upon tongues or lips or voices. Instead, they use their feelers.

The bees and ants are always under strict rule and orders are given and passed on by "touch." You may often see these insects touching each other with their feelers, and you know that they are holding a conversation in their own language.

The birds have certain calls of their own, apart from their songs, which help them to "talk" to each other. They have many warning signals when danger is at hand, which the other birds know and respond to at once. Even the hen has a special call when she wants to bring her chickens back to the safety of her wings. Often, too, we see birds sitting together on a branch having a "chatter." In their own way they are talking over the news of the day.

### Do animals ever change their clothes?

Most animals put on warmer coats in winter to protect them from the cold. Their fur grows thicker and longer, and sometimes changes colour, so that they can hide more easily in snowy weather.

The hare has a greyish coat in winter, and the mountain hare, whose home is in the hills in Scotland, puts on a white coat to blend with the snow.

In his winter dress the stoat is known as the ermine. In northern regions the fox, too, puts on a white winter coat, which helps him to hide from his enemies and to steal on his prey without being seen.

### What is a plumb line?

When you next pass a place where houses or other buildings are being put up, go to the man laying the bricks and ask him to show you his plumb line.

Walls, doorposts, and window frames must be perfectly upright, so the mason holds his plumb line against the wall, post or frame, to test if it is straight.

The plumb line is just a piece of string with a weight (called a plumb bob) on the end. If held up, the string, pulled tight by the plumb bob, hangs straight down, or, as we say, *vertically*. Sometimes the line is fixed to one end of a long plank or board, with a hole cut all along its length. When the board is put against the wall, the bob will be dead in the middle of the hole at the bottom of the board if the wall is upright.

Without a plumb line the builder could not be sure he was building his wall correctly.

### Where does chocolate come from?

The chocolate which we all like so much once grew on a tree. It is made from the cocoa bean which grows on the cocoa tree in warm countries across the sea.

The cocoa tree grows to about the size of an apple tree. When it is from five to seven years old it begins to bear fruit. Thousands of flowers blossom on the tree, but only about a dozen yield ripe cocoa pods.

Every pod contains two or three dozen cocoa beans. The pods are cut open and the beans taken out and dried. Six or seven acres of cocoa trees are needed to produce a ton of dried beans.

The cocoa beans are sent to a chocolate factory to be cleaned and roasted. Then they are cracked and ground down into a chocolate powder. They are then sweetened and flavoured and kneaded into paste. This is placed in moulds and made into bars.

### What blind insect builds a skyscraper?

The most skilful and busy workers of the insect world are the white ants, or termites, as they are sometimes called. Their homes, which we call ant-hills, are often as high as 40 feet.

These queer little ants are blind and most of them are wingless, yet, in spite of these difficulties, they carry through their task with great speed.

They first mix a paste of earthy matter with their saliva, and then these clever builders begin to erect a home so firm and complete that it cannot be broken into without the aid of a pick.

Inside, a large family—perhaps of a million members—finds a home. All the time they are busy making tunnels, adding to their fortress, and finding food. Though they are so small and seem so helpless, yet they lead very busy lives, and are doing good work in helping to fertilise the soil.

Some people, however, do not like termites. They have very big appetites and live on wood. They have been known to invade a house and eat their way inside a table or chair so that only a thin shell, ready to collapse, is left.

### Why do we get a lump in the throat?

Sometimes you hear people say that some fright or sudden shock made "a lump come in their throat."

Does this really happen? No lump really comes in the throat in times of shock, but there is a feeling that a lump is there.

The stomach has some very sensitive nerves and muscles. Thus, when the stomach does not want the food you eat, it throws it back again, and you are sick. In the throat are rings of muscle that squeeze down to the stomach the food you eat. They squeeze downwards at such times, but when you are sick they squeeze upwards.

Now when you have a shock, or are upset or frightened, there is first a queer feeling in the stomach. Then the muscles in the throat, acting as they would if the stomach was sending back unwanted food, work upwards. This working of the throat muscles makes a feeling of a lump in the throat.

*Photos :]* [*Will F. Taylor*

The beginnings of a bar of chocolate are shown in the above photographs. The fruit of the cocoa tree is being gathered by the natives of Ecuador. On the right we have a view of ripe cocoa pods on the tree. Cocoa is an important food, and good chocolate is nourishing.

A fine study of a Chinese boy printer setting up type. Note the sizes of the types in the cases. The Chinese do not use separate letters, but instead employ intricate drawings or "characters" illustrating the words or phrases. In olden times the Chinese knew how to print from movable types. They used this method long before John Gutenberg introduced it into Europe in the fifteenth century.

# WHAT IS IT?—CAN YOU GUESS

Photos:]

1.—Look carefully at this photograph. Examine the background as well as the foreground. What is it?

[Mondiale

2.—This design, so pleasing in effect, is one of Nature's making. Can you guess what it is?

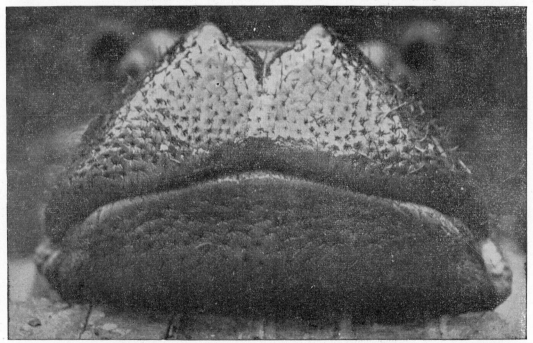

[Mondiale

3—This is not a very difficult problem, if you look closely. It is an interesting sideline for the amateur photographer, to snap objects and scenes from unusual angles. The results are always entertaining and sometimes puzzling. What does the above queer-angle snap represent?

(*Answers on page* 158)

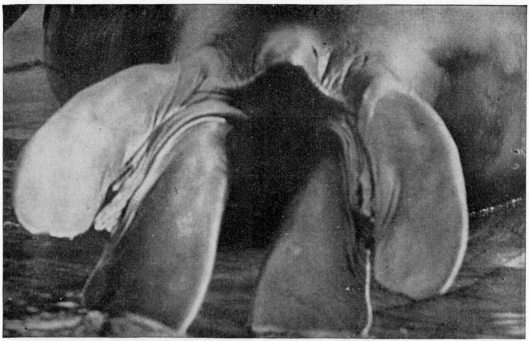

[*Mondiale*

4.—Yes, this photograph is printed right way up! Can you guess what it is? It might help you in your guess to know that it is the rear end of a mammal. But what is the name of the mammal? Another clue is that he is the largest member of his family, and may be as much as 21 feet long.

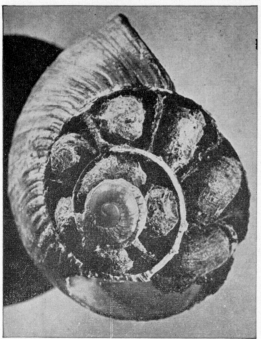

*Photos :*]                                                                                                                                     [*Mondiale*

5.—This may at first seem to be an easy one to guess. Look carefully, though, before making up your mind, as to what the answer to the problem is.

6.—Rather terrible, is it not? Can you guess what kind of a creature this is? He is known to be a "killer," and is very destructive.

(*Answers on page* 158)

Photos :]                                          [Mondiale

7.—What is the matter with this forlorn little fellow?
Where does he come from and why is he dressed in
such a peculiar way?

8.—Is this man playing a game? No, he is working
at his ordinary daily work. Can you guess where he is,
and what he is doing?

Photos :]                                          [Mondiale

9.—Who is this queer-looking creature? He seems
either very angry or endeavouring to reach a top note.
Do you know his name and where he lives?

10.—What is this African holding? Certainly he looks
as though his task is one demanding serious thought
and a great deal of concentration.

*Answers on page* 158

# WHAT IS IT?—CAN YOU GUESS?

## PUZZLE PHOTOGRAPHS

ANSWERS TO PUZZLES on pages 155, 156, 157

❉ ❉ ❉ ❉ ❉ ❉ ❉

1. This is a photograph taken at one end of a native bridge woven in ratan cane, in the form of a long tube. It stretches across the Dihang river, on the frontier of Assam. The tube is four feet in diameter, and it spans a river gulch 600 feet across. You can see the bridge vanishing into the jungle in the distance. This is truly a remarkable feat of native engineering.

2. The centre of a sunflower has here been photographed, showing the multitude of seeds. In one flower-head of this large flower there are 2300 seeds. The sunflower is really a North American plant, but it is also grown extensively in Russia. Oilcake made from sunflowers is used for feeding cattle and poultry.

3. This queer object is a hippopotamus. You can see his huge nose and mouth, and only faintly, out of focus in the photograph, his eyes. The hippopotamus, or "river horse"— though his nearest relative is the pig—inhabits the larger African rivers. He weighs at least 3 tons, and has an enormous mouth with strong, dangerous-looking teeth. He is a vegetarian, living on aquatic plants, and spends much of his time floating in the river with his nostrils and eyes just above water, and the rest of him submerged.

4. These curious flappers are the feet of a Sea Elephant, snapped as he was diving into the water. He belongs to the Seal family, but has two characteristics that earn him his name. He is the largest of the family, a bull Sea Elephant often being 21 feet long, and his nose is a flexible kind of trunk. There are two kinds, the Northern Sea Elephant and the Southern, the latter being the larger animals. They have been remorselessly hunted for the valuable oil obtained from them and now they are becoming rare, especially in the north.

5. Yes, this is a section of a snail's shell. But what are those balls inside it? They are the cells where wild bees are being hatched out.

The wall bee is a solitary type of bee, and seeks out empty shells where her eggs may be laid. Note how each egg is sealed off in a compartment of its own. Most types of bees are solitary, though the honey bee we know best lives in colonies which are a model of organisation and efficiency.

6. A fierce fellow is this! He is the Saga Locust, or Horse-headed Locust. The locust is a scourge. With his never-satisfied appetite and his strong jaws, he comes in his millions across the fertile fields, leaving no green leaf or blade of grass after he has passed. In Africa especially the locust is fought by aeroplane, scientist and farmer. The breeding grounds are sprayed with "killer," while all kinds of traps are set for the ravaging locusts.

7. This pathetic little child is being taken by his father to the Niang-Niang festival, in Manchukuo. The boy has been ill and is now better, so he has had his face painted red, white and black, has been dressed in a yellow coat, and is setting out to give thanks at the shrine of the gods. The Niang-Niang festival is really the Farmer's Festival. The paint used on the child's face is to protect him from evil spirits.

8. This picture shows a coin-tester at work in the Royal Mint, where our money is made. Every coin must be bounced on the block and must ring true, or it is discarded.

9. This big-eyed, open-mouthed piece of ill-temper is a young ostrich, informing mother that it is time she brought in the dinner. In another part of this book you will see what this young bird looked like when newly hatched. A fully-grown ostrich may be 8 feet high and may weigh 300 lb., that is, over 20 stones.

10. The African native in the photograph is holding two ostrich eggs. These eggs have shells so thick and strong that the African natives often use them as drinking vessels.

According to the Arabs, the date palm must have its feet in water and its head in fire. Modern date-growers have taken pains to carry this out. They have also protected the fruit against rain by fixing " umbrellas " above it.

# SCIENCE AIDS THE DATE

## by HAROLD J. SHEPSTONE, F.R.G.S.

ONE of the most popular of winter fruits is the date. Until fairly recently it has come to us from the East, chiefly from the groves in Algeria, Egypt, and around Basra in Iraq. Now America has gone in for date cultivation on a wholesale scale and in a thoroughly up-to-date manner. One reason for this is because the medical profession has endorsed the date as a particularly valuable food-fruit, being rich in protein.

As a result, date groves have sprung up all over Western America, in California, Arizona, Texas and Nevada, the yield being about 25,000,000 lbs. weight of fruit a year. Although in its native home in the East the date palm would appear to flourish with very little attention on the part of man, the American growers found it necessary to carry out lengthy experiments before they hit upon the right methods of cultivation.

The palms in the American groves were grown from suckers obtained in Algeria. As they struggled upwards their growth and habits were carefully watched. Clocks and measuring devices recorded daily growth in split millimetres. As a result many little-known facts about the palm were learned. It grows at night and sleeps during the day. Below 46 deg. Fahr., it hibernates, but when warmed in the spring by the sun's rays, it takes on once more the job of living and producing.

The Arabs say that the date palm must have its feet in water and its head in fire. This is literally true. They require far more water than any other fruit or crop, and it must be delivered to their roots. The groves in fact require attention throughout the year. The first job of the grower is to cut away the sharp, vicious thorns that appear every year on the inner leaf stems. This is essential to enable the growers to carry out the necessary business of pollination and to gather the fruit when ripe.

159

[H. J. Shepstone

This flourishing date-grove in California has been irrigated by water channels. The trees have been scientifically treated, so that they will yield a large harvest of fine fruit. In this way Nature has been helped to better herself.

There are pollen-bearing palms and flower-bearing palms. None of the latter can produce fruit unless their flowers are pollinated. In their wild state there are as many pollen-bearing trees as there are flower-bearing trees and the pollen is carried to the flowers by the wind. The modern grower does not wish to encumber his grove with too many pollen-bearing trees, so he resorts to artificial pollination. Pollen-dipped cotton balls are either applied to the flowers or else these are dusted with loose pollen.

When clusters of fruit begin to appear a heavy paper covering is placed over them as a protection against rain. When the fruit is ready for picking a narrow platform is built around the tree which is reached from the ground by a ladder, and it is from this platform that the fruit is gathered. A good picker will gather from 400 to 800 lbs. of fruit in a day, depending upon how many dates are ripe. As the fruit is picked it is sent to the packing houses. Here it is dusted by passing through a cylinder containing a number of miniature brushes, after which it is washed in a solution which is poisonous to insects but harmless to man, and lastly it is graded and packed.

Photos:]
[H. J. Shepstone

The fruit is gathered from a platform built round the tree. Experts gather from 400-800 lbs. a day. It is then sent to a packing-house to be dusted, washed, graded and packed.

The baby antelope had to learn to fend for itself almost as soon as born, but the young chimpanzee was carried by his mother for quite a while.

# SELF-HELPFUL ANIMALS

### *by* L. R. BRIGHTWELL, F.Z.S.

EVERYBODY knows what is meant by a self-helpful person. We say he can "paddle his own canoe," or that he "always falls on his feet." About a hundred years ago, before a great statesman called Lord Shaftesbury put a stop to child labour, poor little boys and girls were often made to work in factories or the fields when they should still have been at school or at play. It made them very self-helpful, but old when they should have been young, and we may be glad it has all come to an end. Even to-day in tropical countries, where people grow up much more quickly than they do in the north, boys and girls take to work at a very early age, almost as soon as they can walk. In Burma, "toddlers" take the huge water buffaloes out to graze, and even look after them when they help to plough the rice fields. And of course most of us have seen the film about Sabu. That is a true picture of life in many parts of India and Siam, where boys of six or seven help to look after the elephants, and assist their fathers to teach the great beasts how to work.

But with the "lower animals" (that is, all the other animals except human beings), self-help is not just a matter of climate. There are many reasons why some animals fend for themselves when others of the same age are lying snug in the nest and being looked after by their parents. Let us look at two animals everybody knows . . . the cat and the horse.

A new-born kitten is blind, naked and help-less. Even its ears are stuck down flat to its head. For some days it can only crawl on its knees and elbows, like a human baby. It has only two ideas . . . milk and sleep. For some months after it is well furred and has a good set of teeth and claws, it can only play at hunting and catching mice and birds. It has to learn how to get its own living, and if left in this halfway stage of its life would very likely starve.

What a contrast to this is the baby horse, or foal, as it is called. A new-born foal is about as big as a St. Bernard dog. Its eyes are open and it has a good coat of very soft, fine hair. For an hour or so after it has come into the world it lies on one side, quite helpless. Then it begins to struggle to "find its legs." These are so long and thick, and its body is so small that its knees knock against its elbows, and at every attempt to stand it does really "fall over itself." But stand it must, for mother has no idea of trying to feed it by lying down beside it and letting it crawl to its milk like a kitten. So after a bad half-hour or so of struggling and staggering, baby horse gets his first meal. After that every meal becomes easier and the end of his first day on earth sees him able to lollop after his mother at a fair pace.

Thoughtless people take such wonderful happenings for granted. They say it is "Nature" or "Instinct," which of course tells us nothing at all. It is much wiser and far more fun to puzzle out the reasons for such things. That is the only way to learn about animals and to be able to understand them. Why should the cat, and all such flesh-eating beasts as lions, dogs, wolves, weasels, and even seals, be helpless at birth, and grass-eating creatures like the horse, zebra, ox, deer and antelope be able to get on to their feet and follow their parents from the very first?

The answer to this question takes us back quite twenty million years. That sounds a bold thing to say. How do we know anything of the kind could have happened? Well, the men of science are now able to tell roughly the ages of the different kinds of rocks. It follows then that they can also guess the ages, in fact they can "date" the fossils found in those rocks. Fossils, as you know, are just the bones and other remains turned to stone . . . of animals that were once as much alive as you or me. Plants can also become fossils. If then we have a very large number of these fossils and can arrange them in their right order . . . like the kings and queens of England . . . we shall get a fair, rough and ready picture of the changes that have taken place during a very long time, thousands, even millions of years.

So it comes about that we can say quite truthfully some twenty or more millions of years ago the world was much warmer than it is to-day. Larch and birch trees grew in Greenland, and tropical palm trees were flourishing in England. Only the North and South Poles were really cold at that time. Huge steamy forests like those in Burma spread over a great part of the world, not, as now, just between the tropic belts which you see marked on a globe or in the Atlas. Only at the North and South Poles was it really

*Photos :]*                                                        *[Mondiale*

The tiny elephant, already on its feet, is only four hours old, but already moves about knowingly.
       Note the long legs of the baby zebra. Its safety often depends solely upon its speed.

[Mondiale
Though the elephant looks so lumbering and clumsy, he can be cautious in his movements when " small fry "
are about, especially if they are special friends of his, like the goats in the picture.

cold. So most of the beasts which were the ancestors of the modern cats, wolves, horses and antelopes were forest dwellers.

But the world is always changing. After a time great volcanoes and earthquakes forced upwards huge masses of land, until they were much higher than they had ever been before. They rose up into cooler air, and as a result a great many forest lakes and rivers were drained of their water. The tropical plants could no longer live on such cool high ground. But the tough grasses could still live, and soon land which had once been tropical jungle became prairie . . . like the great grass plains we all know from seeing cowboy films. To meet this change of affairs many of the plant-eaters had to change also. Of course many animals, like many plants, perished. But others made the best of things. They moved out into

the open country and managed to live by cropping dry grass instead of browsing on juicy leaves.

Climate and food have much to do with all the different kinds of people we see in the world to-day. Climate and food also go a long way in forming the shapes and habits of the lower animals. All the changes that came over the plant-eaters we need not bother with here, but change they undoubtedly did. The flesh-eaters on the other hand, though they too changed a good deal, remained much more like their ancestors than did the others. You see they always had plenty of meat, they just went on eating the plant-eaters as before, so there was less need for them to change their general ways of life.

Once the grass is eaten in a particular spot there is nothing for the plant-eating animals to do but to move on to the next patch. So the leaf-eaters (now turned grass-eaters) were always on the move, with the fear of the fierce flesh-eating beasts behind them. At one time great parts of Europe and Asia were full of herds of wild horses, deer, elephants, and many other creatures always in search of more and more grass. To-day there live in the Sudan great tribes of wandering cattle farmers . . . like the famous Hausa tribe that spends the year round driving flocks and herds from one pasture and water-hole to another. The Hausas pack up their tiny children and carry them, but a horse or goat cannot pick up its toddler as can a man or even a cat. So the grass-eating animals' babies must toddle after their parents from the very first or lie down and die, and this makes them very self-helpful indeed. The goats' babies or kids can be so self-helpful as to be rather a nuisance. Some at the London Zoo were always climbing out of their yards, and would break into store-rooms, even climbing upstairs and trying to open tins of biscuits with their teeth.

IN a way then we might be tempted to think of the horse as a wiser beast than the cat. It seems more "ahead" of it. It can look after itself so much earlier. But really the rather sheltered life of puss is an advantage. A cat is more intelligent than a horse. It spends longer at school learning from its parents, while the young horse is wandering with the herd like a grown-up. When at last the young cat is told very plainly by its parents that it must go out into the world and hunt for itself, it is a quick-witted beast with lots of strength and energy stored up, and so has a good start in life. It is much the same with ourselves. The longer we can stay at school, so much the better for us when schooldays are done.

Of course there are exceptions to this rule. The hare is a first cousin to the rabbit, but for some reason it has chosen a life in the open instead of clinging to deep banks and the sheltered edges of woods, as does the rabbit. So while Baby Bun is born blind and helpless, Baby Hare has its eyes open and wears a good fur coat from the beginning. Its nest is only a hollow or "form" out on a plain or hillside, and the little hares, like the young wild horse, must be able to scuttle for safety at a minute's notice should danger . . . such as a stoat or a hawk . . . come their way.

There are some wonderful examples of self-help and helplessness amongst birds. But to understand these better let us first glance at the reptiles. Some very strange reptiles long since turned into fossils are believed to have been the very first ancestors of both beasts and birds. In Australia and New Guinea there are still living some strange beasts, the Duck-mole or Platypus and the Porcupine ant-eater that lay eggs just as do all reptiles, and all birds. (Some reptiles appear to be born alive, but this is because the eggs are hatched inside the parent.) It would seem then that there is more of the reptile about birds than there is about beasts. This helps us to understand the very hard-hearted way some bird mothers treat their young, for no reptiles seem to take any interest in their babies at all. The big snakes called pythons hatch their eggs by coiling round them, and the mother alligator scrapes together a rough heap of leaves in which she lays her eggs. But once the eggs are hatched the young can just fend for themselves or die. Most reptiles, lizards, snakes and tortoises just cover their eggs with sand and then walk off and forget all about them. Luckily for the babies they nearly all live in very hot countries where there are plenty of insects and other small creatures easy to swallow, and so they have no trouble in finding their first meals.

Just as we saw amongst the beasts, so it is amongst the birds. The highest and most intelligent are anything but self-helpful at first. All our song birds, the lovely humming birds, the parrots, crows, owls and birds of prey are at first as helpless as a baby lion, monkey, or man. Most birds that are very clever when grown up are hatched blind, naked and helpless, and spend a long time in the nest before they learn to feed themselves or to fly.

But the birds hatched out in grass jungles or on open beaches must look after themselves almost at once. A baby chick hatched in an incubator soon learns to peck and scratch for itself, though it certainly "gets the knack" as we say, more quickly with a motherly old Biddy hen to guide it. Wild poultry—jungle fowls, pheasants, turkeys, and many others, quickly learn how to run for cover or lie flat and hide themselves amongst grass or stones at the slightest hint of danger. A baby ostrich is as self-helpful as a baby horse and

*Photos :]* [*Mondiale*

An amazing example of a " self-helpful animal "—a Shetland foal only one day old galloping about his new-found world, and (below) nibbling grass. Note the sturdy build of the frolicksome foal. Though only small the Shetland pony is noted for his strength and endurance.

soon learns to trot after its long-legged mother.

Two birds at least are as self-helpful as any reptile. One is the Hoatzin, a bird that looks rather like a guinea fowl with a short crest or top-knot. It lives in the deep jungles of Brazil in South America. Next time you see a table fowl ready for cooking look at its wings. You will see on the knuckle of each quite a long finger. This is of very little use to the bird and soon becomes covered with feathers. This finger and the pointed tip of the wing are really the thumb and first finger of what in reptiles is a five-fingered hand. Now the baby Hoatzin as soon as it is out of the egg not only uses its beak and feet for climbing just

called "mound builders" or "brush turkeys." You can see these birds at work in the London Zoo or at Whipsnade. The cock Brush turkey in spring walks backwards in circles, kicking the fallen leaves as he goes until he raises a mound quite six feet high, many yards round, and often weighing as much as five tons. In this heap several hen turkeys lay their eggs and there they stay until the heat of the sun and the warmth of the rotting plant rubbish hatch them, just as the alligators' eggs are hatched. Then, with none to help them, the baby birds scramble up through the rubbish and into the sunlight. There they are able to feed themselves at once, and even to use

[Mondiale

This brush turkey has built the huge nest on which he is perched, by pushing the vegetation together with his feet.

as a parrot does, but it uses this naked wing finger as well. In fact it can scramble about a tree just like a monkey or a tree lizard. By the time it is fully feathered it loses the use of this wing finger, but being by this time able to fly, there is no longer any fear of falling. The only other bird in the world which we know to have had a wing finger like the Hoatzin is one that must have lived quite two hundred million years ago. Only two fossils of this bird have been found so far. They were dug up in some quarries on the Continent and were found in " lithographic stone " which was used for the lithographic method of printing pictures. This fossil bird when alive had *two* free fingers on each wing knuckle and must have been a very self-helpful creature indeed.

In Australia lives a wonderful race of birds

their wings. A "flying start" indeed, but the baby Brush turkeys are not always so lucky.

In the same jungles live enormous Monitor lizards. These find the Brush turkey mound ready-made and pop their own eggs into it, which saves them the trouble of making a nest for themselves. All might be well if only the baby turkeys hatched first. But the lizards' eggs too often win the hatching race, and since the young lizards are as fierce and hungry as so many little tigers, you can guess what happens. It is a case of self-help with a vengeance, and serves to prove what we said about the baby cat and monkey. The baby who is not too self-helpful but spends a long happy time in the nursery and later at school is usually better off in the end.

Be self-helpful by all means—but not in too great a hurry.

Nomads of the desert. Dwelling in tents and roaming the barren desert, the Bedouin tribes
manage to make a meagre living by rearing livestock.

## The Asian Continent

# THE PEOPLES OF ASIA

ASIA may well have been the cradle of all
civilisation, and perhaps the birthplace of
the human race itself. Fossils of early man
have been dug up in Java, in a cave near
Peking and in Kenya's Rift Valley. The skull
of Peking man was unfortunately lost during
the last war, but he seems to have been one
of the first distinctively human beings to understand the use of fire.

Whether Egyptian civilisation is older than
the remarkable civilisation that sprang up in
the Euphrates Valley has not been finally
decided, but they ran a close race. It is quite
possible that the civilisation of China, which
is not as old, derived originally from the early
peoples of Mesopotamia and Persia. No one
really knows where the Chinese came from,
but they entered their present territory from

the West about 3000 B.C. They were certainly
becoming established along the Hwang-ho
River in 1500 B.C., and at roughly the same
time the Aryans invaded India.

Asia is therefore a great melting-pot of
many races. It stretches from within the
Arctic circle almost to the Equator. It is
divided from Europe by the Ural Mountains;
and a much greater mountain mass cuts off
India from the vast plains to the north.

### THE WANDERING TRIBES SETTLE

Geography has largely decided how the
various peoples were originally distributed.
Cereals were cultivated before 8000 B.C. in
Asia Minor, and this naturally gave rise to the
first permanent buildings and a settled mode
of life. It was necessary for grain to be stored

and measured by simple arithmetic, and for laws to be made to control a more complicated life than that of wandering tribesmen. Tribal society gave way to the city-state and finally to empire.

The growing of crops began along the shores of the great rivers. The domestication of animals, on the other hand, did not necessarily call for a static community life. We know that cattle, pigs, sheep and horses, were domesticated between 8000 and 6000 B.C. The horse originated in Asia and without it there would have been no nomads of the central steppes. It revolutionised warfare and made possible the great invasions which led to such an intermingling of races and religions. The northern peoples of the steppes are yellow-skinned, slant-eyed Mongols. They crossed China and India into the Malayan archipelago and left Islam as their legacy. All the great religions of the world have arisen in the East.

## THE VARIETY OF PEOPLES

We sometimes think of all Asiatics as people with brown or yellow skins, but in such a vast land mass people of every shade of complexion can be found. The Mongol types are yellow, but there are tribes sprinkled from Assam to Formosa who are practically white-skinned. They very possibly survived from a primitive race out of which both Europeans and Mongols emerged. There are white Caucasian traces among the aborigines of Indo-China. On the other hand, some of the aborigines of southeast Asia are black.

A more reliable way of classifying different races is by their hair and shape of head. The Negritos, who are to be found in parts of Indonesia and the Philippines, are woolly-haired and very dark. The Mongols have straight hair and round heads. The Malays are long-headed with wavy hair. But pure types have been to a great extent either submerged or dispersed. There are, for example, 136 different peoples in Burma alone. Needless to say, there are a great many different languages, although the majority spoken on the mainland belong to the Tibeto-Chinese

A tribal meeting in Mongolia. In the foreground are three Lama priests. Derived from Buddhism, Lamaism has been corrupted by the introduction of ceremonies of magic and divination.

family and consist of words of one syllable which change their meaning according to the tone in which they are uttered.

## HOW THE PEOPLES LIVE

If you look at a map of Asia, you will see a vast but thinly populated territory between the Arctic Ocean in the North and the Himalayas in the South. The Samoyeds, and other primitives in the Arctic region, eke out a livelihood by hunting and fishing. Across the whole of Northern Siberia, there is a treeless zone called the tundra. Here, too, life is harsh and the inhabitants depend mainly on reindeer, which they use for food, transport, and clothing. In the forest belt to the south, trappers trade in furs, much as in Canada. There are, however, exceedingly valuable regions of black earth, particularly in the neighbourhood of Omsk and Semipalatinsk, where excellent crops can be cultivated. The Soviet Government has spent large sums of money on experiments of growing wheat farther north, but the result is not yet certain.

## ASIATIC RUSSIA

Very little information is available about recent development of the mineral resources of Asiatic Russia. Gold has long been mined in the Yenisei Basin. There are considerable deposits of magnetic iron and coal in the region of Kaznetsk, and platinum has been found at Pitsk. Now, as in the past, Siberia is partly colonised by political prisoners. The deplorable conditions in the mines and the appalling climate have made it a place of punishment. But new lines of communication are opening up—for example, the railway which links the black earth grain-growing zone with the cotton-fields of the Central Asiatic Republics—and a transformation is taking place.

There are textile factories in Uzbekistan; and here, and elsewhere, tribesmen, who until a short time ago wandered as nomads, are being turned into factory workers.

## MANCHURIA'S WEALTH

The Republics of Mongolia are still largely in the pastoral stage. Manchuria is rich in forest and minerals. Its steppes have been an attraction for the past hundred years to emigrants from the overcrowded provinces of North China. These wide, open spaces, which

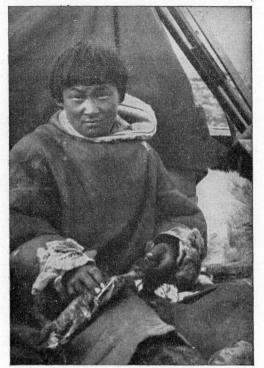

This Samoyed fisherman is warmly clad against the bitterly cold Siberian wind.

continue into the central grasslands, have been developed in modern times by the construction of railways. The largest single crop is the soya bean, but wheat is grown in increasing quantities. A further source of wealth (and also of trouble) has been the discovery of coal and iron in South Manchuria. Japan badly needed both, hence its wars with China. Between Mongolia and Tibet lie the barren lands and the Gobi desert. This desolate region contrasts with the two most densely populated countries in the world—China and India.

## THE INDIAN SUB-CONTINENT

Three-quarters of the enormous population of India work in connection with the land, and this is both India's strength and weakness. A good harvest depends on the monsoon rains, and when these fail, there is famine, and millions may die of starvation. The level of industrial production is so low that India cannot make adequate use of its raw materials. Coal is found in Bengal, the Central Provinces, and Hyderabad, and there are deposits throughout most of the sub-continent yet to be exploited. There are oilfields in Assam and the Punjab, but so far no wells to equal those of Burma.

At one time, the diamond mines of Golconda were world-famous, but these have been exhausted. To-day, India sells her wheat, rice, cotton, and jute, for manufactured cotton goods, machinery, sugar and oil. The results of under-development are the great extremes of poverty and wealth.

The Punjab is one of the granaries of the world, but the chief Indian crop is rice, which is the staple food of most of the people. Primitive methods of agriculture are still used, and the Indian peasant is not easily adapted to new ways. The caste system, which perpetuated rigid class divisions and a whole population of ' untouchables ' was abolished by law in 1949 but had not been eradicated in practice and has made it more difficult to enter the modern world. An equally sharp barrier separates Hindus and Moslems.

It is impossible to speak of an Indian race, or even language. There are so many languages that educated Indians usually employ English as a common medium for private and official purposes. Sanskrit is as dead as Latin and

A young Hindu from Kashmir with his caste mark on his forehead.

classical Greek, but there are a number of words in both these so similar to their Sanskrit equivalents that it is clear that the Aryan invaders spoke a language from which nearly all European languages have also evolved.

## THE CHINESE

China has an even bigger population than India, and also suffers gravely from industrial under-development. The people belong roughly to two physical types—those of the north being tall and long-headed, and those of the south smaller and round-headed. They have yellowish skins and the Mongolian eye-fold. Four-fifths of the population speak Mandarin, but there are very many local dialects. Like the Indians, they are mainly dependent on agriculture and subject to terrible famine when the rice crops fail.

In Europe, it takes two acres to support one person, but in China five persons have to live on the produce of that amount of land. Nevertheless, the Chinese are skilful farmers and they work extremely hard. The richest soil is along the Yangtze. This is one of the best agricultural regions in the world and feeds nearly half the population of China. In addition to rice, it grows barley, wheat, beans and peas.

There is wisdom and kindness in the face of this old Arab shepherd

A Chinese farmer with his granddaughter. The thickly-padded clothes worn by the child are brightly coloured.

In the north, where the climate is colder, the people live on wheat and millet, and such meat as they can afford. But in spite of the very high annual production of rice, China cannot adequately support its population, and has to import from Indo-China, Thailand, and Korea.

The Chinese have overflowed into many parts of Asia and are particularly numerous in Malaya and Singapore. The great silk trade

Chinese children in Hong Kong enjoy a game of ping-pong on the pavement.

is no longer a monopoly of China, and India has captured the English tea market. But China has now embarked on a drastic programme of industrialisation similar to that undertaken in the nineteenth century by Japan, This industrial revolution in China is under Communist control.

## THE JAPANESE

The Japanese resemble in appearance the more stocky physical types of South China. They have straight, black hair and are of Mongolian extraction. There are also traces of mixture with the primitive Ainus whom they

Fishermen of the Ainu race, the original inhabitants of Japan.

displaced. Their mountainous volcanic islands do not grow enough food to support the expanding population. The problem was intensified when Japan adopted Western techniques. In order to keep its factories going, it needed coal and iron from Manchuria, tin, copper, and rubber from Malaya, oil from Indonesia, and the surplus rice of Burma, Siam, and Indo-China. The attempt to conquer these lands and build up a great Japanese empire ended in the catastrophic defeat of 1945.

## TROPICAL ASIA

With the exception of Ceylon and Burma, tropical Asia is the most backward part of the

Young Fiji Islanders at work on a banana plantation in Suva.

A Tongan chief and his wife. Though of high rank and entitled to special clothing, they wear a piece of matting over their clothes as a symbol of humility.

continent. The islands of the Pacific still contain some of the most primitive peoples in the world. The only absolutely pure race is found on the Andaman Islands. The Melanesians, who can be found from New Guinea to New Caledonia, and the Polynesians from Samoa to Hawaii, have intermingled.

Strictly speaking, like so many other classifications, Malay is a language rather than a race. It is spoken by a brown-skinned people, who excel as sailors. The Pacific islanders include many different types from black-skinned pygmy Negritos, to tall Papuans and woolly-haired Fijians. Some are savages practising head-hunting and even cannibalism; others live like the food gatherers of the Stone Age.

## WESTERN ASIA

To come back now to Western Asia, where civilisation began, we find that once flourishing cities are buried under sand. The Fertile

Men of the Fiji police force wearing their distinctive serrated-edge skirts.

Farmworkers of Antioch, now known as Antakya, in the South of Turkey. Although the main cities of Turkey have been westernised, life in the rural districts remains little changed.

Crescent that grew such abundant crops for the ancient world and ran from the Euphrates through Palestine to the Nile, has become partly a desert. But a new source of wealth has been discovered in Persia, Iraq, and Arabia—oil.

Arab tribesmen still lead a nomadic existence, but the camel is rivalled by the motor lorry and aeroplane. Persia, now called Iran—the word means Aryan—and Iraq, are being driven into the modern world. Turkey entered it very determinedly after the downfall of its Empire in 1918.

## ASIA'S FUTURE

Obviously, we can no longer talk of the unchanging East, for the traditional way of life is rapidly altering. The peoples of Asia are no longer resigned to an inferior status. They have become aware that the superiority of the West is due to its science, and that this can be learned and applied by themselves. Every conceivable level of society from Neolithic times onwards is still to be found in Asia. But there are now startling contrasts and amazing transformations. Although tribesmen still roam the Central plains, many of them can see films and listen to the radio, and with the advance of education children of primitive tent-dwellers are becoming skilled mechanics and even scientists.

Asia is rich in natural resources that have yet to be exploited. It also has a limitless reserve of manpower. It is impossible to exaggerate the significance of bringing these two together—especially if the search for uranium now going on is successful, and atomic energy becomes available for those countries with a shortage of coal. That will be the biggest revolution of all.

The building skill of the Mayas can be seen in these ruins in Yucatan, Mexico.

# THE NATIVES OF THE AMERICAS
## The First Inhabitants

UNTIL the end of the last Ice Age there were no human beings anywhere in the American Continent. All the evidence we possess suggests that man first entered America from Siberia. Between 10,000 and 20,000 years ago, the retreating ice sheet was followed by a mass movement of game to the north of Siberia. This naturally attracted the hunters and they crossed the Bering Straits into Alaska. They found themselves in an enormous virgin territory, a veritable hunters' paradise. Their descendants gradually drifted to the south across forests and prairies, penetrating the jungles of the Equator and reaching beyond to the pampas of Argentina. The whole migration took thousands of years, starting from the Arctic and ending on the fringe of the Antarctic.

It used to be thought that all these prehistoric peoples belonged to a single race akin to the Mongols, and that they split up into various sub-races with different languages derived from a common root. Recent discoveries, however, show that the truth is much more complicated. Some languages in South America are like those of the original inhabitants of Australia and are not in any way related to the languages of North America. It is probable, therefore, that there may have been a small scale migration from the Pacific not less than six thousand years ago.

### NOMADS AND SETTLERS

The overall picture is of Stone Age hunters spreading across the Americas, some settling down to village life, but the majority depending mainly on the chase. There are striking exceptions in Mexico and Peru, where powerful Empires grew up at about the time of our own Middle Ages. They built impressive towns and had a complex social organisation. The gold with which they loaded their temples was fabulous and ultimately brought about their downfall, but the extraordinary fact remains that although they advanced so far in some directions they still relied mainly on stone tools and weapons.

Apart from Peru and Mexico and the Pueblo communities of Arizona and New Mexico, the natives of the Americas did not live in towns. Those who remained in the Arctic adapted themselves, like the Eskimos of to-day, to the bitter climate and long dark winters. They lived by hunting and fishing. Life was scarcely less rigorous for those who ventured into the Canadian forests. Their chief food supply was moose and caribou and they used the skins of these and the smaller animals that they trapped for making clothes and tents.

Conditions were much easier for the natives who settled along the north-west coast. Fish and game were plentiful and a more static existence was possible. They developed a remarkable skill in woodwork and made canoes by hollowing the giant cedar trees. Sometimes these canoes reached 100 feet in length, and, for graceful design, they have no equal in the world.

### THE REDSKINS' FOREBEARS

The tribes who moved into the vast plains of the interior were the forerunners of the warlike Redskins encountered by the white pioneers when they opened up the West. We can imagine their delighted surprise when they had their first glimpse of herds of bison grazing on the short grass. Deer, elk, and antelope were also plentiful and it must have seemed a Happy Hunting Ground. They made up for their lack of weapons by organising mass attacks on the herds. The bison were stampeded by setting the grass on fire and either trapped in a corral or driven over the edge of a cliff. Hunting on the plains became much easier after the Spaniards introduced the horse.

### AGRICULTURE DESPISED

A Stone Age people can only practise agriculture successfully in the most favourable circumstances. Very little can be done in forest regions, but on the plains maize was cultivated by crude methods. There were, of course, no ploughs or draught-animals, although domesticated dogs were used to carry small loads. The staple diet on the plains consisted of maize, beans, and buffalo meat. Agriculture was despised as a woman's occupation and the men

of the tribe centred their lives on the chase. Before qualifying as a " brave " the youths of the tribe underwent a painful ordeal of initiation.

### THE PUEBLOS

The most advanced culture in North America was reached by the Pueblos of Arizona, New Mexico, Nevada, and Colorado. It was started by a long-headed people who discovered the art of basket-making about 2000 B.C. Their descendants learned how to irrigate the land and began to build villages with houses of stone or adobe (sun-baked clay). While the Indians of the plains and forests did not advance, the Pueblos made steady progress. By the year A.D. 700 they had improved their pottery and learned how to weave their clothes from cotton. Quite large towns had been built by the eleventh century with houses several stories high. They evolved a complex social system and religion. This was a peaceful urban civilisation surrounded by savages who made periodic raids.

### THE MAYA CIVILISATION

But the Pueblos had not reached the highest level of the various aboriginals who moved across the Continent. The Mayas of Central America far surpassed any achievement in the North. Their Empire spread over Guatemala, Yucatan, south-east Mexico, and western Honduras. The ruins of their temples still excite wonder, and most astonishing of all is the calendar they devised.

No one knows how they acquired such a knowledge of mathematics and astronomy and quite fantastic theories have been put forward to the effect that the Mayas were survivors of the lost continents of Atlantis and Mu.

### THE TOLTECS AND AZTECS

They built cities with populations of 30,000 and 40,000 each. They were conquered by the Toltecs who came from the northern plateau of Mexico between A.D. 600 and 1100. The Toltecs were in turn conquered in the fourteenth century by the Aztecs, who also came from the north. They were a warrior people, far more brutal than the Mayas. Prisoners of war were sacrificed and the climax of all their resplendent religious ceremonies was the ritual killing of a victim.

They built imposing stone temples with

A Mexican family outside their adobe hut. The old walls have lost their protective coat of mortar and are beginning to crumble away. There are, of course, big cities in Mexico where conditions are identical with those in big cities everywhere, but in the country districts more primitive conditions, such as these, are to be found.

great staircases on the outside leading to the place of sacrifice. Sometimes the heart of the victim was cut out with a flint knife, and sometimes he was flayed alive and the priest would put on his skin. Ceremonial cannibalism was also practised.

The Aztecs prized jade more than gold, which they merely regarded as an ornament, since they did not use money. It was their gold, however, that the Spaniards coveted, and

Cortes brought this bizarre civilisation to an end in 1520. Despite its cruelties, it had some fine artistic achievements to its credit. Incidentally we can be grateful to the Aztecs for chocolate—the word itself is derived from their language.

## THE SPANISH CONQUEST

It has been estimated that at the time of the Spanish conquest, there were over eight

Two little Mexican girls wear their mantillas when they go to church.

A Mexican boy dressed like his father as he rides to a rodeo.

A street vendor, whose ancestry is part Indian and part Spanish.

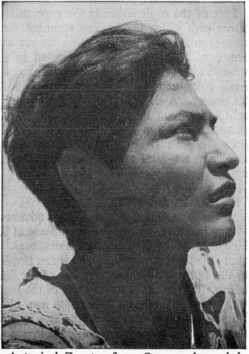

A typical Zapotec from Oaxaca, descended from some of the earliest " Americans."

Carnival time means dressing up and fun and laughter to this little girl.

Lake Titicaca to Ecuador, with Cuzco as the capital. Their social system was a kind of communism. All the land and its produce were owned by the State. There were no private employers and practically no trade in the ordinary sense. Labour was conscripted for agriculture, road-making, the mines, and so on. All produce was pooled and distributed to the various sections of the population in certain fixed proportions. When a new piece of territory had to be opened up, the government did not hesitate to deport whole populations. For a modern parallel, we can take the Russian system, but of course there were many important differences.

The state socialism of the Incas did not pretend to be in the interests of the workers. It could only be operated by a large body of officials who constituted a mandarin class. It was for them to decide what public works should be undertaken, how big a labour force was required, and how a surplus of maize, for example, should be distributed. Their authority was derived from the fiction that the King or Inca was literally a god living on earth. Like the Pharaohs of ancient Egypt and the Emperors of Japan, his divinity was related to the sun. Also like the Pharaohs, he had to marry his sister.

## THE CULTURES OF EGYPT AND PERU

The various resemblances to Egypt have led some anthropologists to speculate about the possible diffusion of the culture of the Nile valley across the Pacific via Easter Island to the coast of Peru, where in fact, the first centres of a higher civilisation appeared. Some support to this theory is also given by the practice of mummifying the dead. The mummies of the ruling Incas were preserved in the Temple of the Sun at Cuzco, where they were found by the Spaniards.

Opponents of diffusion hold that similar cults and ideas can spring up independently. There is nothing surprising in sun-worship, and the custom of preserving bodies of the dead may have arisen in the highlands of Peru and Bolivia, just as in Egypt, because it was noticed that in such a dry atmosphere corpses did not decay. The question has not been finally decided, but the majority opinion to-day is that the Incas developed their beliefs on their own account.

million Indians in Central America, and one of the mysteries of history is how Cortes managed to overthrow the powerful Aztec Empire with a force of only four hundred men.

Part of the explanation is the superstitious terror with which the Indians regarded these strange white invaders riding on horses and armed with guns. This was reflected in the weakness and vacillation of Montezuma, the Aztec ruler, and it undermined the morale of his armies. A deeper reason was the lack of cohesion among the various city states that comprised the Empire. They were torn by jealousies and rivalries and felt no strong loyalty to a central administration which had only kept them together by force.

## THE INCAS OF PERU

In South America an even more advanced culture had been attained by the Indians in the highlands of Peru. Its origin goes back to about the third century B.C., and it ran parallel to the Maya civilisation. We have very little information about the forerunners of the Incas who began to dominate Peru about A.D. 1100. It is impossible to assign precise dates because the Incas, unlike the Mayas, did not invent an accurate calendar.

They created a large Empire stretching from

Toltec relics, showing the advanced state of carving of the people who preceded the Aztecs.

## THE INCA CIVILISATION

They grew maize and potatoes in the fertile valleys, and domesticated the llama and alpaca. As weavers, they have never been excelled. The craftsmen who made textiles out of cotton or wool, like the potters and metal-workers, were given a fixed amount of raw material by the State and told what to produce. Under such a regimented system individuality was not encouraged, and it is all the more surprising that art should flourish.

Inca pottery was of excellent quality and extremely rich in colour, but, like the Mayas and Aztecs, the Incas were ignorant of the potter's wheel. They produced exquisite work in gold, tin, copper, silver, and platinum, and yet primarily they remained a Stone Age people.

They had a complete mastery of every type of stone building. Hundreds of miles of stone terracing still exist in the Andes valleys built for agricultural purposes. Paved roads and cable bridges comprised an admirable system of communications. Professional couriers enabled the hierarchy of officials throughout the Empire to keep in touch with one another.

## THE SPANIARDS VICTORIOUS

But there was a fatal flaw in this marvellous organisation, as Pizarro discovered soon after he landed on the coast of Peru in 1527. The belief that they were ruled by a god in human form was the mainspring of the elaborate organisation of governors and officials who supervised every form of production in the interests of the State. The Spaniards arrived at a lucky moment when a pretender to the throne had kidnapped the chief Inca and tried to take his place. Pizarro took the pretender prisoner and the chief Inca was murdered. The Empire was suddenly bereft of a divine ruler in the midst of a foreign invasion. The whole machinery of this closely integrated State came to an abrupt standstill. The victorious Spaniards plundered the gold and enslaved the bewildered population.

## THE PRIMITIVE TRIBES

Nowhere else in South America was there anything to compare with the Inca civilisation. Most of the scattered tribes practised some sort of agriculture although they led a very primitive life in the tropical jungles and in Patagonia. The general pattern was much the same as in North America. Nomads lived in temporary shelters in the forests, but on the open plains, where they hunted game, they made use of skin tents.

The most distinctive weapon of South America was the blow gun with darts poisoned with curare. The tribes of the pampas hunted the guanaco and ostrich with a weapon consisting of two stones attached to a cord, called the bolas. The bow was widely used in almost all regions except in the Andes. North American Indians scalped their enemies, but from Colombia to Peru, and especially in

An Huichole Indian chief in full " regalia " comes to town with an attendant. He holds his prized possession, a violin, in a rather unorthodox manner.

Ecuador, the whole head was required as a trophy, and the curious practice arose of shrinking human heads.

## THE KON-TIKI THEORY

Until very recently it was not thought possible that the culture and techniques of America could have been exported before the arrival of Europeans. A theory was advanced, however, that the islands of Polynesia were first occupied by the predecessors of the Incas at about A.D. 500 and that a still later immigration reached the islands from Peru in A.D. 1100. It was thought that this would explain certain similarities of legends and the baffling monoliths on Easter Island.

The chief objection to this theory was that the Peruvians could not have made such a journey by sea. Their only craft was a raft made of balsa wood and it seemed impossible that early mariners could have survived the storms of the Pacific. However, Thor Heyerdahl and five Norwegian companions built an exact replica of the ancient Inca balsa raft and made a daring 4,300 mile journey from Peru to Polynesia, and certainly established the feasibility of what is now known as the Kon-Tiki theory—the name being taken from the chief god of the Polynesians.

An Indian woman in Pisac, Peru, wears her Sunday best on special occasions.

# OUR RIGHT TO VOTE

IN the time of George III the members of Parliament formed themselves into two main groups—Whigs and Tories. The Tories were mainly " the King's friends " and supported his attempt to get personal power. Of the Whigs, some—though by no means all—were reformers who wanted to change the way of electing the House of Commons so that it really would represent the wishes of the people.

During the Napoleonic wars and afterwards, the Tories were in power. It was they who, seeing the bloodshed and disturbances of the French revolution, were afraid of reform and were opposed to change. Their rule was oppressive and restricted people's liberty. The Whigs therefore became popular because some of them spoke for greater freedom and for real representation of the people in Parliament.

The House of Commons in Sir Robert Walpole's administration.

## BROADENING THE FRANCHISE

In 1832, the Whigs, in spite of the difficulties of bribery and " pocket boroughs," where parliamentary representation was in the hands of a single individual or family, won a general election and were able to get a majority of the House of Commons to agree to a great Reform Bill. Under the old system, the members of Parliament came mostly from the farming districts or from ancient market towns. Great new towns like Manchester and Birmingham had no borough corporation and elected no M.P. The Whigs' Reform Bill had two main objects: first, to abolish " pocket boroughs " and to distribute the membership of the House of Commons more equally over the country according to the population of each district; second, to give the right to vote (or franchise) to owners of land or houses of a certain value. The great majority of the common people were still to have no vote, but in every district there would now be far too many electors for any rich man to bribe.

The House of Commons passed the Bill, because the Whigs were in the majority there; but the House of Lords threw the Bill out. It could not become law unless both Houses agreed to it. The deadlock caused great disturbances throughout the country. There were huge and noisy public meetings and some rioting in the streets. The Whig Ministers were able to persuade the King, William IV, that to prevent serious trouble he would have to create enough new lords of Whig opinion to ensure that the Bill would pass the House of Lords. This would have meant that the Whigs would have had a majority in the House of Lords for a very long time. The threat of it was enough, and the Tory Lords gave way. This event showed that, of the two Houses of Parliament, the House of Commons was becoming the more important.

## THE CHARTISTS

So the great Reform Act became law and a new method of electing the House of Commons cleared the way for more changes. The common people thought these first reforms were not enough. A group of working men, following the idea of Magna Carta, drew up a " People's Charter " demanding a vote for all men over twenty-one, an election every year, and payment of salaries to M.P.'s so that working men could be elected. All over the country there were meetings of many thousands of working people who supported the Charter (and so were called the " Chartists.") They signed their names on a great petition to be presented to Parliament. The reforms they asked for were too much even for the Whigs to accept, and the Chartists struggled in vain to persuade Parliament to grant their demands. By 1850, after fifteen years of struggle, the Chartist agitation died away, but the movement towards reform went on. Nearly all the points of their Charter are now part of the law of England. The Reform Act of 1832 had settled the principle that members of Parliament should represent the people, and gradually, by more Acts of Parliament passed in 1867, 1918, 1945 and 1948, the right to vote was extended until every man and woman in the country is able to vote both for Parliament and for local councils.

## GROWING POWER OF COMMONS

After 1832, nearly all members of Parliament belonged to one of the two great political parties.

The party which gained the majority of votes at a general election became the party in power. As the House of Commons came more and more to be truly representative of the people, it became the rule that King (or Queen, as at present, and in the case of Queen Victoria, whose reign covered most of the 19th century) should choose Ministers— that is the Government—from the party which had the majority in the House of Commons, so that " His Majesty's Government " was in sympathy with the feelings of the people throughout the country. Queen Victoria at times objected to having to choose Ministers whom she personally disliked or disagreed with; but she had to give in. For if her Ministers, chosen, as they might be, from either the Lords or the Commons, had not a majority to support them in the House of Commons, it would have been impossible for them to govern the country. No laws could be passed without the consent of the Commons, nor could any taxes be raised to pay for the Army, Navy and other public services. It was essential, then, that the Ministers should be chosen from the party which had won the last general election. As a result of all this the personal power of the King or Queen to decide how the country was to be governed rapidly declined.

This method of choosing a government from one or other of two great political parties has gone on for over 100 years, though the names of the parties have changed. The Whigs and Tories of 1832 became Liberals and Conservatives in Queen Victoria's time. After 1900, when most working men had the right to vote, they wanted a party of their own, and Labour appeared as a third party in elections. In recent years, most people who want great changes and sweeping reforms have voted for this party. The two-party system now works with Labour in place of Liberals. Smaller parties support sometimes one, sometimes the other, of the two big ones.

## THE ACT OF 1911

Until 1911 there was another difficulty. In everything but the control of money, the House of Lords had equal power with the House of Commons. When the two Houses disagreed, and neither would give way, it was usual for the King to dissolve Parliament and a general election to be held. If the result of the election showed that the country disagreed with the House of Lords, that House usually gave way; but sometimes they did not, and then the only course was for the King's Ministers to ask him to make enough new peers to change the majority in the House of Lords. This was rather inconvenient. If done often it would have made the House of Lords (composed of hereditary and not elected members) into a body of enormous size.

Accordingly, in 1911, the House of Commons, which then had a Liberal majority, proposed a new law which said that any Bill which the House of Commons wanted should, after two years, and if passed by them three times, become law whether the House of Lords had agreed to it or not.

The Lords resisted this, and King George V was advised by his Liberal Ministers to use the threat of making new lords. As in 1832,

A speech by Lord Gordon in 1780 provoked the Gordon Riots in which catholic houses were looted and burned.

the House of Lords gave way before the threat was carried out. The new law—the Parliament Act, 1911—was passed, and the result now is that the House of Commons is supreme and the House of Lords is no longer equal in power.

## LOCAL GOVERNMENT DEVELOPMENTS

Side by side with the reform of the national government, reforms took place in local government. There was no great disagreement between the political parties over these reforms. Before 1835 there had been little effective local government. In the chartered towns there were the elected corporations, but the electors were few, and consisted chiefly of property owners or " freemen " whose right to vote depended on ancient rules and customs. Outside these towns were the counties, each of which was divided into parishes. The inhabitants of each parish met in the vestry and appointed overseers of the poor and overseers of highways. Each inhabitant had to pay a contribution, or rate, towards the upkeep of the poor and the roads. The parishes in the county were supervised by the Justices of the Peace, who were magistrates appointed by the King from among the local gentry. These Justices appointed the parish constables, and had power to deal with minor crimes. The Justices of the Peace for each county were therefore the local governing body for the county, and the vestries were the local authorities for the parishes. The work done was not very effective. The borough corporations were corrupt and negligent, and the vestries and the Justices, not wanting to pay high rates, provided little in public services. Roads and sanitation were bad; there was no public education or health service.

## INDUSTRIAL CLAIMS

In 1835 the borough corporations were reformed; more people were allowed to vote; and the corporations were given greater powers to provide local services. England at this time was becoming more industrialised, the towns were growing bigger, dirtier and more overcrowded. To avoid the spread of disease, and to help industry and trade to grow there was need of better provision for public health, education, poor relief and roads.

Special boards were set up to deal with these various matters. First there were Boards of Guardians to attend to the relief of the poor; there were Highway Boards for the roads; School Boards to provide free education; Boards of Health to deal with disease; and Sanitary Authorities, each with a Medical Officer of Health, to look after water supply and sanitation. All these boards were elected and charged rates upon the local inhabitants.

## DIVISION OF SERVICES

So many different boards and other authorities, including the Justices of the Peace, the borough corporations and the parish vestries,

Westminster Hall was built in 1099. It was the chief seat of the law for centuries, witnessing the trials of many great men.

each with their different areas, led to some confusion. It has all been much simplified since then. The various boards and the vestries have been abolished, and the Justices have few powers except to hold courts of justice. The local authority for each county is an elected county council; each borough has an elected borough council. The counties are divided into county districts each of which has an elected council; each rural parish has a parish council or a parish meeting. These local authorities carry on local services such as education, roads, town-planning, parks, housing schemes, sanitation and fire brigades.

Side by side with the local services are the nationalised services such as the post office, labour exchanges, hospitals, electricity supply and railways. As Parliament came to represent the people, so it concerned itself more with the well-being of the people and with the provision of these various " social services."

# DEEP DIVERS

IF one were to dive too deeply into the depths of the sea, the tremendous weight and pressure of the water would crush the frame of the body. Yet queer creatures live at enormous depths and are only very rarely seen by man. By specialised structure of their forms they are able to withstand the great pressure. But there are some surface creatures, mammals too, like the whales, which can safely go down to very great depths. Such divers have specially developed lungs in which they are able to retain air and they can rise to the surface without having suffered harm.

When hunted and wounded, frantic whales probably dive to even greater depths. At any rate they feed half a mile below the surface, remaining down some time. The pressure there will be 1,250 lb. to the square inch yet the peculiar " sacs " of sperm oil which seal the nostrils when under water prevent the air in the lungs from being forced out. If it were otherwise the whale would suffocate.

As a rule a man can hold his breath for about a minute only, though with practice he can remain under water up to about five minutes. Instances are rare however. The seal is a better diver, and is able to remain down about fifteen minutes, the fin and humpback whales up to half an hour; while the bottle-nose and sperm whales have been known to stay more than an hour below—and remember, in considering this feat, that they are mammals, not fish.

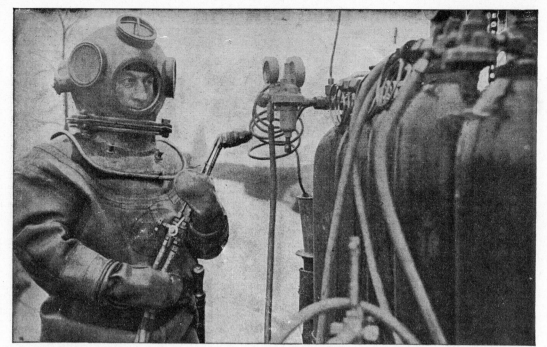

[*Mondiale*

A number of oxygen containers are necessary for long work under water. The diver holds the autogene flame cutter in his hand. It is lit, and the diver descends into the water.

# FLAMES UNDER WATER

## *by* J. E. PRYDE-HUGHES, F.R.G.S.

ONE of the most difficult tasks which come the diver's way is that of cutting through iron and steel plates under water. This work, which is involved in the raising of sunken ships or removing wrecks and other obstacles to shipping, could, hitherto, be done only with comparatively primitive tools. The diver deep below the surface of the water had to cut through the stout metal with a steel hand-saw. As the work had to be done oft-times at considerable depth, the diver's strength and endurance were quickly exhausted. The rate of progress was very slow—a yard or so of the side of a ship cut through in several hours.

Now the modern methods employed enable rapid progress, cause less exhaustion, and assure the completion of repair work which otherwise would be impossible without further expensive operations.

Before the war the autogene flame-cutter made its appearance. Its success in enabling a fierce flame to be used under water, was quickly recognised, and the process developed.

By means of this cutter a tremendously hot spurt of flame is directed on the iron or steel which has to be cut—the metal at the cut becoming molten. Ordinarily this would be impossible under water, but a remarkable invention, which was further developed during wartime and became of immense value to the country, enabled the difficulties to be overcome, and the diver in the deep sea is now enormously relieved in his arduous job. The ability to utilise a flame under water naturally revolutionised repair work. To-day, the diver, instead of spending hours of heavy labour with a hand-saw, takes a burner in his hand, and sinks below the surface of the water, just as if he were on dry land. With his modern apparatus, he melts a cut several millimetres deep in the iron or steel wall to be repaired or removed. The cutting proceeds rapidly. In ten to twelve minutes a stout iron plate a yard long can be cut through, and besides, the diver does not use up his energy as he used to do, for the cutting-flame does the work for him.

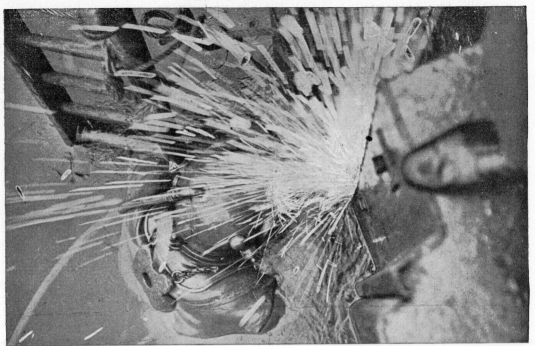

Photos:]                                                                                                  [Mondiale
The flame is alight under water. Its heat is over 3000 degrees Celsius, and it must be held well away from the diver's or the diving-suit would be destroyed. In this case, the diver's job is to cut through an iron sluice gate.

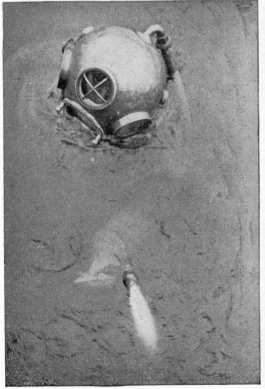

The discovery of a method whereby the effects of water on flame were avoided was really a piece of genius. At first the method was to protect the flame, which is of enormous heat—up to 3500° Centigrade—by means of a hood, that is a mantle through which compressed air is forced with such pressure that the water is driven away from the path of the flame. Without this protection the water would, of course, rush in and overwhelm the flame. But ingenuity went a step farther. The hood became superfluous with the most modern electric methods.

THE needs of war led to a broadening of the invention's scope and the apparatus was improved accordingly. Technical development marched on apace. Early attempts at underwater welding by means of an electric arc were made with the use of a diving bell, and met with some success. But there was lack of efficiency in view of the obstacles to be overcome. Then the gas blowpipe fitted with a surrounding shield which stuck to the side of a ship, acting rather like the vacuum rubber cup, proved not entirely satisfactory, for the operator could not see well what he was doing, and the "sucker" shield failed when uneven surfaces were met with. The electric arc with a mechanical screen also had its disadvantages, not so much in the maintenance of the electric arc as from the depositing of the metal from the electrodes. Eventually these various inconveniences of the earlier methods of underwater welding were overcome by the Peillon process. Experiment and experience had shown that the maintenance of a stable electric arc under water creates a highly efficient shield of metallic vapour which completely insulates the water from the actual arc. This factor gave the answer to the problem of effective underwater welding, and to-day the electric welder operates universally on all manner of metal repairs and salvage deep below the surface, in docks and locks, in lakes, rivers and the open sea. Not long ago it was thought impossible to keep a light burning in water, but now it is quite easy to do so.

For many years normal welding in the air was, in America, conducted with uncoated mild steel electrodes, in Great Britain (and later in U.S.A. also) flux-coated electrodes have been usually employed. Such electrodes could not, however, be used for underwater work because of electrolytic action, so a special flux coating had to be provided, one which contained an insulating varnish. This is an additional precaution against electric shock, for though the ordinary rubber diving suit should protect the operator, a defect might develop with resulting danger to the diver but for the insulation of the electrodes and holder.

The men who utilise these new methods of welding and salvage work are skilled operators. One has but to note the elaborate technical kit to realise this. The whole underwater world one might say, constitutes their field of action. The first application which leaps to mind is the repair of ships, and during the war and the period after its conclusion there was much to be done in this sphere. With the new processes it was, fortunately, no longer necessary to tow a damaged ship to port and dry-dock it for examination and repair. In many instances the damage could be attended to, even when plates had to be cut and replaced, at sea. When bomb, torpedo and mine created such havoc amongst the merchant ships which braved the dangers of elements and war to bring to this country the food which was essential to maintain our health and strength to work and fight, and the munitions, oil and other important things necessary for the prosecution of hostilities, many a stricken vessel was rendered seaworthy again in as many hours as previously it had taken days or weeks, by the employment of the up-to-date diver-welder. What this meant to our power to maintain the struggle only those with intimate knowledge of the events knew, but undoubtedly this new invention was a great factor in keeping sufficient ships at sea.

There are many other ways of use for the underwater flame cutter and welder, in salvage work, the underwater parts of great dams, in bridge building, tunnelling, on dock gates and buoys which have to be maintained serviceable, on piers, breakwaters, sluices, quaysides, pipelines, and a host of other places. Underwater works all need repair and attention from time to time and after accidents, and so it can be seen what an enormous value there is in the ability to maintain a fierce cutting flame in water, and how the once difficult and onerous labour is rendered comparatively simple by the new processes described.

# GREAT BELLS OF THE WORLD

## by ERNEST MORRIS

The great bell " Kolokol," in a courtyard of the Kremlin, Moscow, is the largest bell in the world. It weighs 193 tons.

BELLS vary in size from quite little ones like the old-fashioned door-bells, to real bell monsters weighing many tons. The big bells are known by the Latin name *signa*, and on the Continent of Europe as *bourdon* or base bells.

The largest bell in the world is now in the Kremlin at Moscow. Just imagine yourself standing by this great giant "Kolokol," or "King of Bells," as it is called. Its height would reach as high as a two-storey house, for it is twenty feet and on a pedestal. It is twenty-two feet eight inches across, and was made over two hundred years ago, in 1733, and it weighs 193 tons. This great bell replaced another which was broken in a fire of 1701, and like that bell, it, too, was broken in a fire.

Just after it was cast, a great fire broke out and destroyed much of the city and reached the Kremlin. The heat of the fire and the throwing on of cold water caused the bell to crack. It lay in the earth for over a century, but was eventually raised and placed on a pedestal, where it now rests in the courtyard of the Kremlin. The broken piece—eleven tons in weight—has been placed nearby so that people may easily see inside.

Besides this great bell, Russia has many others of great size. At St. John's Church, Moscow, is one of ninety-six tons, and there is another in the same city called " Bolshoi " (big) which weighs about sixty-four tons. St. Isaac's Cathedral, Leningrad, has a famous set of eleven big bells, the largest being twenty-nine tons.

In the East there are some very big bells, but these are quite unlike our Western ones. They generally are of a bee-hive shape, without a lip or "sound-bow," and in all cases are rung —not by an *inside* clapper or tongue—but struck from the *outside* by a rammer, usually a great baulk of wood, often the trunk of a tree. This is swung on ropes or chains with great force to a "boss" on the bell.

The great bell of Peking weighs fifty-three tons. It was made over 2,000 years ago and is still bright and sound. So beautifully is it cast, that it is easy to read the 8,000 Chinese characters engraved upon it both outside and inside. In Nanking is a similar bell of twenty-two tons.

Japan has many big bells and gongs of great age, splendidly made. The best-known are at Kyoto and Mudera. Some are ten feet high and adorned with sacred texts from Buddhist Scriptures. The greatest bell of Japan is that of Chion-in and this is seventy-four tons in weight.

An even bigger bell is at Mandalay, Burma. It is at the huge pagoda at Mingoon. This monster is in the open air and suspended on three massive round logs of teak placed horizontally one over the other, their ends resting on two pillars of great size. It is one of the biggest hanging bells in the world.

On the Continent of Europe most of the big bells, or *bourdons*, are not rung like the smaller ones, by wheels or levers and ropes, but by the treadle or see-saw fashion. Usually two

long planks of wood are placed across the head-stock of the bell and set at right angles to it. The ringers go up over these and by their feet push the bell this way and that—forward and backward—like a giant see-saw.

In some instances, like the Great Bell of Notre Dame in Paris, the arrangement is like a platform which, when the bell is at rest, completely covers the pit. The heaviest bells usually require four men, two on either side, and sometimes more, to manipulate them.

In Europe—apart from Russia—there are no bells of such great size, but you should remember that these great Eastern and the Russian ones do not swing, but are struck either from the outside or are sounded by pulling the clapper to the bell.

The great bell of Cologne Cathedral, which replaced an old one dated 1448, weighs 25 tons, and that of Lisbon Cathedral 21 tons; while the big bell of Montmartre, Paris, is 20 tons. There was one at Olmutz of 18 tons and another at Vienna of $17\frac{3}{4}$ tons. The famous bell of Erfurt, dating from the fifteenth century, is also $17\frac{3}{4}$ tons and is over 10 feet high and $8\frac{1}{2}$ feet across the mouth. Many other cities in Europe have big bells of over 10 tons.

[E. Morris

A Japanese fourteenth century Temple Bell at Uji.

[Hulton Picture Library          [Fox

Here are famous bells indeed. On the left are the bells of Big Ben at Westminster, heard all over the world on the radio. On the right are the bells of St. Paul's.

[E.N.A.

St. Paul's Cathedral, London, Christopher Wren's masterpiece. On the previous page you have seen some of its chime of twelve bells. One of these, "Great Paul," is England's largest bell.

The largest bell ever cast in England is the bourdon of the huge carillon of 72 bells now at Riverside Church, New York, U.S.A. This is 18¼ tons and is made to swing by two electric motors placed on the bell frame. These pull in opposite directions and swing this giant frame high. It has a similar companion, also cast in England (at Croydon, Surrey), the bourdon of 72 bells at Chicago University. This is 17 tons, and these carillons are the greatest in the world.

England's largest bell is "Great Paul" of St. Paul's Cathedral, London, and this was made at Loughborough in 1881 and it weighs 16¾ tons. This bell you may hear every day (except Sunday) at one o'clock for about four minutes, when it is raised about frame high— or half-way up—by four members of the cathedral staff. These men time their pulling with great precision, the first stroke of Great Paul being heard within a second of the clock striking.

The clock bell is named "Big Tom" and weighs 5 tons 4 cwts., and there are two quarter bells of 24 and 12 cwts. "Big Tom" is tolled only for the death of a member of the Royal Family; for a Bishop of London;

the Lord Mayor or the Dean. These bells are in the right-hand tower as you look at St. Paul's from the west end, the one with the clock-face. In the other tower, on the left or north side, is the great peal of twelve ringing bells with a tenor bell of 62 cwts. This is the third heaviest of its kind, Exeter Cathedral having a tenor of 72½ cwts., while the new Anglican Cathedral of Liverpool has a ring with the biggest bell weighing 82 cwts.

Next to Great Paul comes Great George of Liverpool, which is 14¼ tons. You will note all these big bells have names. They are so-called after either their donors or the church to which they belong.

"Grandison" of Exeter, the tenor just referred to, was so-named after the Bishop who gave it in 1360. Another big bell at Exeter is called "Great Peter" and was the gift of Bishop Peter Courteney in 1484, and this weighs about 4 tons. Other "Great Peters" are at Gloucester (2 tons 18 cwt.) and York Minster (10¾ tons), this latter being the fourth largest bell in England. Two famous "Great Toms" are at Lincoln Cathedral (5 tons 8 cwt.) and Oxford. This last one hangs in the gateway tower of Christ Church called "Tom

THE 'BOURDON' FOR THE LAURA SPELMAN
ROCKEFELLER MEMORIAL CARILLON,
RIVERSIDE CHURCH, NEW YORK.
NETT WEIGHT—AFTER TUNING— TONS. CWTS. QRS. lbs.
18 - 5 - 1 - 18.
THE LARGEST BELL EVER CAST IN ENGLAND.
GILLETT & JOHNSTON, CROYDON, ENG. FEB. 1928.

[*E. Morris*

Tower," and is rung nightly at 9 p.m. to call the students home. It weighs 6 tons 4½ cwt.

"Great John" of Beverley is 7 tons, while "Little John" of the Nottingham Exchange buildings is 10 tons 7 cwt. There is a famous bell at Tong, Shropshire, originally given by Sir Henry Vernon in 1518 to be tolled whenever a Vernon came to Tong. It has twice been recast and now weighs 2¾ tons.

Bristol University has a big bell called "Great George" of 9½ tons, and there is a great bell named "Hosannah" set amid twelve smaller ringing bells at Buckfast Abbey, Devon. This is 7½ tons, while a similar arrangement is at Newcastle Cathedral, where the "Major" of nearly 6 tons, rests above the ordinary ring of twelve bells. Also arranged in this way are the bells of Worcester Cathedral, where the great bell of 4¼ tons keeps company with sixteen others. Many of Britain's town halls have big bells to strike the hours; at Manchester the bell weighs over 8 tons; Preston nearly 5 tons; Bradford 4¼ tons; Bolton and Leeds over 4 tons.

But perhaps the most famous of all bells, and certainly the one whose voice is most familiar, is "Big Ben" of the Houses of Parliament, London. He was one of the earliest broadcasters, and people all over the world have set their clocks and watches to his stroke. He was named after Sir Benjamin Hall, who was First Commissioner of Works in 1856.

The following list gives the weights of the biggest bells in the world:

| | Date | Tons | Cwt. | Diameter ft. | in. |
|---|---|---|---|---|---|
| Moscow ("Kolokol") | 1733 | 193 | 0 | 22 | 8 |
| Trotzkoi, Russia | 1746 | 171 | 0 | — | – |
| Moscow | 1817 | 110 | 0 | 18 | 0 |
| Mandalay, Burma (Mingoon) | 1780 | 87 | 0 | 16 | 4 |
| Chion-in, Japan | — | 74 | 0 | — | – |
| Moscow (Wspenski) | 1760 | 63 | 8 | — | – |
| Moscow (St. Ivan's Church) | — | 57 | 1 | 15 | 0 |
| Peking | — | 53 | 0 | — | – |
| Rangoon, Burma ("Shway Dagohn") | 1840 | 42 | 5 | — | – |
| Novgarod | — | 31 | 0 | — | – |
| St. Petersburg (Leningrad) (St. Isaac) | — | 29 | 0 | 11 | 0 |
| Moscow | 1878 | 28 | 13 | — | – |
| Cologne Cathedral. Kaiserglock (SW. Tower) destroyed 1914-18 to make munitions of war, replaced 1925 | 1874 | 25 | 0 | 11 | 2 |
| Nanking, China | 14— | 22 | 0 | — | – |
| Lisbon | — | 21 | 0 | — | – |
| Kyoto, Japan | — | 20 | 0 | 10 | 0 |
| Paris (Montmartre) | 1898 | 19 | 8 | 9 | 11½ |
| Rouen Cathedral. "Jeanne d'Arc," destroyed 1944 | 1914 | 18 | 6 | — | – |
| New York City, U.S.A. Riverside Drive Church | 1931 | 18 | 5 | 10 | 2 |
| Olmutz, Moravia | 1931 | 17 | 18 | — | – |
| Vienna (Emperor Bell), destroyed 1914-18 to make munitions of war | 1710 | 17 | 17½ | 9 | 10 |
| Moscow | — | 17 | 16 | — | – |
| Toledo, Spain | — | 17 | 0 | — | – |
| Chicago University | 1932 | 17 | 0 | 9 | 9 |
| London ("Great Paul," St. Paul's Cathedral) | 1881 | 16 | 15 | 9 | 6½ |
| Rouen Cathedral (Ambroise, destroyed 1793) | 1501 | 16 | 1 | 10 | 8 |
| St. Petersburg (Leningrad, St. Isaac, second) | — | 16 | 0 | 9 | 4 |
| Philadelphia, U.S.A. (John Wanamaker Store) | — | 15 | 11 | 9 | 6 |
| Liverpool ("Great George") | 1937 | 14 | 10 | 9 | 6 |
| London (Westminster "Big Ben") | 1858 | 13 | 11 | 9 | 0 |